ALL THE THINGS LEFT UNSAID

Michael Harding is an author and playwright. A recipient of the Stewart Parker Award for theatre, a Hennessy Award for Short Stories and a Bank of Ireland/RTÉ award for Excellence in the Arts in 1990, he has written numerous plays for the Abbey Theatre and was writer in association with the National Theatre in 1993.

His novels include *Bird in the Snow*, *The Trouble with Sarah Gullion* and *Priest*. He is also the author of several bestselling memoirs including *Staring at Lakes* (winner of the Bord Gáis Energy Book of the Year award), *Hanging with the Elephant*, *Talking to Strangers*, *On Tuesdays I'm a Buddhist*, *Chest Pain* and *What is Beautiful in the Sky*.

He is a member of Aosdána, a columnist for over fifteen years with *The Irish Times* and his podcasts are available on the Patreon platform.

MICHAEL HARDING

all the THINGS left UNSAID

HACHETTE
BOOKS
IRELAND

First published in 2022 by Hachette Books Ireland

Copyright © Michael Harding 2022

First published in paperback in 2023

A CIP catalogue record for this title is available from the British Library.

The opening stanza of 'To a Blackbird' by Patrick Kavanagh is reprinted
from *Collected Poems*, edited by Antoinette Quinn (Allen Lane, 2004),
by kind permission of the Trustees of the Estate of the late
Katherine B. Kavanagh, through the Jonathan Williams Literary Agency.

ISBN: 9781529379204

Typeset in Apple Garamond and Adobe Garamond Pro by
Bookends Publishing Services, Dublin

Printed and bound in Great Britain by Clays Ltd, Elcograf, S.p.A.

Hachette Books Ireland policy is to use papers that are natural,
renewable and recyclable products and made from wood grown
in sustainable forests. The logging and manufacturing processes
are expected to conform to the environmental regulations
of the country of origin.

Hachette Books Ireland
8 Castlecourt Centre, Castleknock, Dublin 15, Ireland

A division of Hachette UK Ltd
338 Euston Road, London NW1 3BH

www.hachettebooksireland.ie

For all the old friends whose lives enriched me
so wonderfully. And for all their loved ones,
who endure the loss.

Their names remain in the heart.

Some of the people mentioned within this book
are well known but other names and
identifying details have been changed

CONTENTS

JUNE 2020

The first text I sent was like a warning when I reread it.

   I fell on the beach today.

Then I fell a second time two days later. After limping back to the car, I texted the same friend.

   Alone on the beach. And another fall. Bad omens.

But I didn't press the 'send' button. There are parts of me I never like to share in written words. I suppose that's what makes me a writer.

JUNE 2021

One year and two operations later; I had been in Beaumont hospital twice in the space of six months for operations on the spine that might have left me in a wheelchair or incontinent or just dead, and having been restored to health by the hands of so many gifted doctors and nurses, I felt a kind of inundation of light. I could only describe it as an intimate experience. An encounter. I don't want to say religious experience because that might put you off.

It was a transformation not of my own making. I can't adequately relate how terrified I was of hospital, of scalpels and knives and ink marks on my eyebrow and marks all along my spine and tight surgical socks and hospital gowns that tied up at the back. I didn't like one bit of it. Though I pretended I was not bothered. I hid under the blankets. I sheltered beneath the soft voices in my earphones. I counted every day like a decade until I was free.

One day a friend phoned. I saw his name on the screen and decided not to answer.

Then he called again. This time I did pick up.

'How are you?'

'I'm fine,' says I. 'How are you?'

He went on to talk about the immediate reason for his call. Someone we both knew when we were students had died. I expressed sadness, and then went on to talk about the old days, politics, various television programmes, and an amount of books that either one or both of us had recently read.

We were almost at the end of the chat when he turned again to me.

'But how are you?' he asked again.

I said actually I'm great but I couldn't talk just now and that I might call him back in a week or so.

He hung up and I wondered what had just happened.

He was a friend. I was in hospital. Yet I never told him. I was feeling dejected, anxious and perhaps slightly depressed. I never told him anything.

'You play your cards very close to your chest,'

someone once said to me years ago, when she couldn't construe what I was thinking.

I had not written to my old school friend for years. Never texted nor phoned. He did all the work. And I suppose it was when I got sick that I noticed it most. I lived with my worries bottled up inside me. He phoned regularly, pouring out his woes, and leaving nothing bottled up. And then he would go on to inquire how I was doing, and I would put up a guard, a shield, a ring of steel, and the conversation became a game to prevent him extracting anything from me.

When you get ill and then recover, a sense of elation overwhelms the body. That's why I went to the coast. Gratitude can be so intense that you need to be alone with it. You need to nurture it. Bring it to the surface and offer it to the gods, to Jesus maybe, or Buddha or whomsoever is your mentor deity. Gratitude is a sensation so beautiful that you almost feel glad that you got sick in the first place.

Not that I was out of the woods. One year and two operations later I was at the coast. I arrived at the end of April and I was still very fragile. But I stood at the edge of the ocean. It was blue. I lay on the sand and I stretched myself to look up. It felt like blue eyes in the blue universe were watching me. Illness had been like an ocean and my body a small boat tossed here and there. Recovery was like finding land safely. Now I was overwhelmed with gratitude, as if the same ocean of suffering had contained a hidden motherly presence. After all, I had survived.

I wanted to give thanks, and the ocean seemed the place that was calling out to me, now tender in its splendour and gentleness.

The wind was in my ears as if someone spoke:

'I can take care of your wound,' the wind seemed to say. 'I can take care of your heart. I can take care of every detail. You must only think of me.'

A comforting message but to whom was I speaking?

'You don't have to tell anyone,' she whispered. 'It can be our secret.'

And that was the first day.

As Rumi says, the wound is where the light comes in.

The beach had been the scene of the crime, because it was there I first noticed things were going wrong with my body. But I was returning to the place of the storm, metaphorically, and acknowledging it as the most beautiful place in the world, on the edge of the ocean in Donegal.

It was here that I'd fallen ill, and I thought it would complete the journey if I returned here to rest. Not to be physically mended, because that had already happened, but rather to be healed in the heart, and to savour the light that was flooding into me in the wake of a sickness that could have finished me off, had it not been for modern medicine.

And it was here that I planned to stay, for a full year, until the spring of 2022, by the water's edge with only occasional visits home to Leitrim, and occasional visitations from the beloved who would come up from Leitrim to mark the seasons, the feast days, the family days, the birthdays and death days. But essentially I was committed to retreat, to an embrace of solitude and to the ocean, to give thanks simply for being alive.

Watching the light every day dance on the waves and the waves fall like thunder on the shoreline and on the rocks along the broken islands around the beach. At night the wind bringing the sea to me in roars that tore the darkness asunder from one Good Friday to the next.

I was released from hospital on Good Friday of 2021 and arrived at the shoreline at the end of April. It was

the beginning of the most wonderful retreat I have
ever embarked on. The beginning of what in Islam
they call the longest spiritual journey a human being
can ever make – the journey from the head to the
heart.

August 2022

I look back now at the old me. The person I was before August 2022. Before the operations. Before I wrote the letters.

For many years the only ash on my face in Lent came from the stove in the studio shed where I lingered for years, and through the lockdowns, like a miner trapped underground, daydreaming about the lovely world that existed outside. I wrote about it. And I felt my way into the world with words and sentences and books. But I lived alone, because I lived without God. And I endured modernity with great melancholy, because I lived only with the memory of God.

Over the years I had privatised my religious practice and eventually my only refuge was my father's bookcase in the corner of the studio, its shelves decked with bells and candles and holy icons. It was a tiny museum of deities, Buddhist and Christian icons, and various artefacts and ritual objects gathered over the years.

I touched each object with nostalgia: the Indian incense holder I bought in the Dandelion Market, the Tibetan water bowls I brought home from Mumbai, and the mala beads that were a gift from a monk in Mongolia. On a separate shelf were three sets of Christian beads.

My mother's beads were made of precious green stones, linked together by an ornate silver chain, and which I called her Laura Ashley rosary because the green of the beads matched the curtains in her bedroom. When she was in the golf club my mother always held her teacup with thumb and forefinger, and when in church she always brought forth the beads from her purse with a flourish of stylish sanctity.

The second rosary on the shelf belonged to my grandmother. The beads were brown and shaped like little orange pips with a grim black crucifix attached. The crucifix contained nothing of the joy that Jesus promised, but instead was charged with a sense of human agony and pain.

And the fact that the beads were once entwined around my grandmother's ivory fingers in death didn't incline me to use them. For me they evoked a time when yellow flypaper hung from every kitchen ceiling, a Tilley lamp lit the way to musty bedrooms, and the toilet was out in the yard.

I wasn't one for reciting the rosary, but maybe I was just superstitious enough to drop one into the bottom of a suitcase whenever I was travelling.

The final set of beads on the shelf were my own. I bought them in a gift shop in Assisi many years ago when I was flitting about Italy with my daughter, hoping that a grand tour of churches and monasteries might imbue her with a sense of awe and admiration for the cultural heritage of the continent. A fanciful notion on my part, although we did end up purchasing lots of holy stuff in the gift shop, because St Francis was very much a lover of animals, and there were sufficient donkeys, birds and fishes in his entourage to impress any eight year old.

A monastic gift shop holds much the same allure as a shopping mall in Tenerife. Instead of handbags, wallets and other leather accessories, there are a hundred types of rosary, and even I couldn't resist the compulsion to purchase something. I chose a rosary that was made of wood and threaded with a simple black cord because its rustic simplicity reminded me of a time when I had friends who played guitar at folk masses and wore sandals.

But you might think that illness would have made me more religious. Instead it did the opposite. I woke to the reality that all my mentor deities and saints and angels were plaster or wooden carvings that sat on shelves gathering dust, and that alone in a room was no way to embrace the mystery of life, no matter what beads you prayed with.

Every week I set out tablets in a seven-day dispenser; pills to stabilise my blood pressure and regulate the heart. My creaking limbs grew heavy with age, and the lockdowns were interrupted only by trips to various hospitals for routine check-ups. I accepted a daily dose of tablets as just another sign of ageing.

I remember heading for town one morning in Leitrim when I saw a neighbour sitting on his roof, lying against the tiles as he stripped plaster off a chimney. I was alarmed at his dexterity and daring, because he was as old as myself.

I opened the car window and observed that it was a fine day.

'The chimney is leaking,' he said. 'The mother sits in the kitchen watching the damp come down the walls, so I have to do something. Don't let the old man in, as they say.'

'Well, at least you're keeping busy,' I suggested.

Although personally I felt that being busy was over-rated. I was in the garden with clippers that afternoon pruning a rose bush, a shrub my mother brought to the house years ago. But after a few moments I fled to a bench, wrapped my coat around me and began brooding, because my mother had crept into my head once again and I needed to sit with her awhile.

It was ten years since she was wrapped in the silence of a Cavan graveyard in 2012. Although during the lockdowns I noticed with curiosity that I was regularly ambushed by a sense of her presence. I no longer saw her in a coffin, or buried in the cold wet clay, and when I went there to stand at the tombstone, occasionally I could no longer connect her presence with the heavy marble monument or the faded plastic flowers in their little glass dome that rested on the white pebble stones of the grave.

Instead I felt her presence in the trees when the wind blew, and in the kitchen when the aroma of apple tart wafted in the air, or indeed on the beach in Bundoran where she, like me, once was ambushed by the joy of youth.

Mother was everywhere as a comforting background noise, or presence.

'Comforting', indeed, was the word I used; as I took my tablets, as I made another journey to outpatients, and as I viewed the endless flow of news about wars and pandemics and unhinged political leaders, in a world where nothing seemed to be at all well.

But comfort wasn't quite enough when I was in hospital.

Like everyone else, I want to hope. I want to defy the bleakness and the grief that gathers around us. Faced with grim outcomes, I began to understand that my salvation lay in others, and that my damnation was at my own hand, every time I closed the door to keep the world at bay.

Does it seem strange that I would then fly to where the land ends and the ocean begins, leave even my beloved behind and walk the beaches for 12 months composing letters and emails of confession and regret?

I suppose yes, it was strange, especially when those I wrote to could not possibly read a word I wrote, apart from my old school friend. Perhaps the only way to make sense of it is to share the letters with you.

And the first of them was to him.

To an Old School Friend

April 2021

Thanks for the text. To be honest, I'm completely fucked. And thanks for the phone calls. You're a great communicator. You're kind of unrelenting sometimes, the way you keep in touch. But it's only now that I appreciate it. I always feel bad when I get a message from you and don't respond. Or sometimes I respond and tell you nothing. I know sometimes I've been on the phone with you for an hour, listening to your woes, and told you nothing, which people might think is kindly but it's also sly. It's a way of hiding.

Whereas you have been so loyal over the years, constantly keeping in touch through emails and phone calls and texting me every chapter of your life story and all your sorrows and joys.

You wanted to know where I have been? Well, I was in hospital at the beginning of 2021. I had an operation to embolise a fistula in the spine. Don't bother looking it up. It was just a leaking pipe that needed to be plugged. They did the job, but it opened up again and then they had to do open surgery on the spine to get at it manually. I think it's fixed now and I'm in Donegal on my own crying like a sore cat. I hope you're okay. I heard your friend died. But at our age we're only biding our time until the next catastrophe.

I moved about the beginning of the year nervous of Covid and in pain, unable to walk much or even bend to pick up clothes off the floor. It was March when I returned to Beaumont for the open surgery on an artery in my spine which they tell me was successful. And afterwards it was all rest and time to heal. Which is why I came here to the ocean. I like the long days of solitude. Just me and the waves. When it's all around me the sea becomes a form of company.

Sometimes I think I might create a comedy show from my failures. A detached retina, a heart attack, colitis and depression. But this last little mischief, this arteriovenous fistula, sending the blood in the wrong direction around my body, it nearly finished me off. If it weren't for the team in Beaumont I'd be dead, or sitting in a wheelchair waiting for my legs to go numb and my guts to die even while I'm alive. So you can guess that I'm actually feeling good. Grateful. And I suppose illness is a rite of passage.

I have begun to see more clearly that something waits for me, for you, for us all, at the end of the corridor. It might be a room or a trolley or a quiet nursing-home day room. And that's if we are lucky to have time before the end. The spinal operation for me was a threshold into fragility. And I welcomed it. No, not because I'm heroic. But it seemed like common sense. There was only one alternative and that was to rage against it. And raging against it would be folly on two levels. Firstly there are so many others suffering so much more than me, that in context my difficulties are trivial. And secondly, I believe that rage would have only made me more uncomfortable.

I don't practise religion. I brood on it. I'm not on any moral high ground philosophically, but from time to time I do recognise that religion can be useful in the way that psychotherapy is useful.

So maybe this illness is the best thing that ever happened to me. It awakened in me a childhood fragility, and when I walk along the beach I experience a strange sense of belonging. It's like joy in the air. I feel loved now more deeply than ever.

I couldn't believe I wrote that last sentence. Yet I pressed 'send' before thinking it through. And then he replied.

You are loved.

And this is another old male I'm emailing. Two silverback gorillas would be more likely to email love poems to each other than us.

But I couldn't stop now.

Let me put it another way. When I was awake at night and the door had opened to all the dark horses, as John Moriarty would say, and when they were stomping around inside me I would leave my open hand on the pillow and imagine it to be in the hand of some saint or other. I'm promiscuous about saints. I don't even categorise them into different religions.

St Bernard, Teresa and Padre Pio sit alongside the glorious buddhas and dakinis and wisdom teachers from all the world religions. There's a beautiful Tibetan practice around what is called the jewel tree, which I have sometimes used. In this practice the meditator sits in a straight position and visualises a great lake, and in the lake there is an island and on the island is a great tree.

This is the tree of wisdom. And on the tree, along its branches from top to bottom, are all the wisdom teachers of the world and through history. And at the top

of the tree is my own particular mentor deity. It might
be Mary, or Jesus, the prophet, blessed be his name, or
a modern Gandhi. It might be one of my beloved friends
who has passed away. It all depends on the mood I'm in.
I love this way to meditate, because it has a personal
dimension; the intimacy of holding in my heart a mentor
deity, and at the same time it has a cosmic dimension
— gathering into one visualisation the entire family of
humanity represented by wisdom teachers from all the
corners of the universe.

I don't even wait to re-read, or check for typos. When
the time comes I just press 'send'. Like diving into the
sea without thinking.

Don't allow yourself to have second thoughts.

Lying in hospital at night while nurses move quietly
around the bed, checking some change in a patient's
blood pressure, or helping relieve someone's pain,
with my face sideways on the pillow, feeling
uncomfortable because of the 30 staples buttoned
down my spine, where they opened my back, I'm
overwhelmed with anxiety, wondering if I'll ever have
the use of my legs again. I put my open hand beside
my face on the pillow and imagine it in another hand,

maybe the hand of the holy mother of God, and in no time at all I am sleeping like a baby. A sense of belonging takes away the pain.

Because anxiety is underpinned by the fear of being alone. And it's only when we are alone that we are forced to find belonging at a deeper level.

The portal is opened.

The parameter of the self is broken down and, despite the stampede of dark horses, there is in me a capacity to reach out, imaginatively, and place an open hand in the hand of the holy mother.

Or sometimes it is the hand of another human being. And sleep comes. I don't do it for philosophical reasons. And not because I care about the ideology of any religion. I don't even do it because it's useful and healing. I just do it because I want to belong.

'Send'.

And it's gone.

And I'm glad. Because I don't care now. I know that healing requires this discipline. Don't think twice. Send it. Say it. Risk it.

I have never spoken like this to anyone. I'm terrified of being caught out by what I say. An old professor of mine would quote the adage *verbum scriptum manet* — as if writing anything down was a mistake because it could catch you out in later life. So I've never written these things. I leave them unsaid. Because it's safer. Which is why I write so few letters. But the illness clarified for me the value of paying attention to others. And paying attention to the imagined others in my soul. The necessity of embodying a relationship with the invisible world and affirming that I belong in the universe in this moment and in this body, by shaping mentor deities with my imagination and speaking to them. These are whispers. These are secrets. These are prayers. Why am I telling you this?

There was no immediate response. I had gone too far.

Maybe you can understand why I'm alone now at the shoreline of the ocean. And why after the illness I wanted to be here alone. And why I talk to you. How I talk to you because I talk to God. And God says, talk to him. Talk to the other humans. And I say, what? I leave the humans to be alone at the shoreline so I can talk to God and God says talk to the humans?

I don't know. As I said earlier, I'm fucked. It's being here alone that brings fragility out in me. And I like that. It's new for me to be this fragile.

So here I am on the beach. I have been here a single moment, an afternoon, but it has lasted four seasons, through summer and winter, here, in the same moment, on and off, attending to the waves, and listening for something.

Between daylight and darkness there is a crack. Between one word and another there is a silence. Between waking and sleeping there is an island. I've been listening for something to come through those cracks. Some whispering from the far end of my little universe. But only when some new illness afflicts me, or touches me, do I really hear the great whispering.

It's like a lover. That's the paradox.

It was Holy Week, 2021. I was daydreaming in the busy ward; consultants and their entourages coming and going to different beds like pilgrims attending to the bones of saints.

I was in bed for a week before they operated, and a week afterwards recovering, with staples in my back and a catheter buried in my bladder. Pain can be destructive but the spaces in between the pain are useful for meditation. The first time they attached a catheter was during the operation. I woke with it already in place. I swam up out of the anaesthetic much weaker than before, my energy depleted from various drugs.

I had not been expecting a catheter.

When I felt it between my legs I was devastated. Not just because of the pain if I moved but because it humiliated me. It's a long rubber tube, transparent so you can see urine passing through, and blood if there is blood. It collects in a bag hung from a hook on the side of the bed. I woke in a transition ward. A teenage boy lay in the bed opposite. He held a teddy bear and wore a funny red hat the staff had given him so he wouldn't scratch his head where they had operated. He was like a clown, or a Christ from a painting by Goya.

I didn't want to look at him. He laughed without reason, as if he were mocking me. Or as if he were being scourged inside. I wondered was he real or just a figment of my imagination.

An emanation of my unconscious self.

The ward was full of patients coming out of theatre. We were all companions, sharing a journey. On the same road. And his devastation, his bleak comic pain, felt like an embodiment of a deeper me.

That is me, I thought as I looked at him.

And then I moved in the bed and discovered the catheter in my bladder for the first time. At least I wasn't paralysed. At least I could feel my legs, and a nurse who came to check the drip said everything had gone well. But the rubber hose between my legs pulled at my innards. The other end of it moved inside my bladder.

Twenty-four hours later they removed it. I was elated.

Not so fast, they said, and they checked my own bladder was functioning. A jelly was rubbed on my stomach and a machine moved across the skin and a nurse watched the numbers rise on the little screen. She didn't look happy.

'I'm afraid it's not good,' she said. 'You are retaining too much fluid. We will try again later.'

She was obsessed with the milliletres my bladder retained every time I tried to pee. Whenever I used the bathroom I alerted her, and she rubbed the jelly on my belly and moved the sonic monitor across the skin and watched the screen.

'It is not good,' she said each time. Finally, she looked at me with some pity. 'We are going to put it back in,' she said.

I had been sentenced. I watched patients get out of bed, and shuffle in their dressing gowns towards the toilet. And I envied all of them. It was midnight when the doctor arrived; a gentle young African, with a white shirt and beautiful hands. It wasn't painful. But the sensation of the tube moving inside demanded my complete attention, and a kind of surrender.

Do you see what I mean by fragility?

It's not the big dramatic things that matter. It's tiny little things that unbalance us; small moments in which we first discover we are fragile, helpless and must let go if we are to find peace. There is no avoiding the institutional arrangements. A doctor is a member of staff. He wears shoes and he goes home when his shift is done. I am an inmate, barefoot on the bed, and I go home when they decide. It's a kind of micro-fragility, yet complete.

I'm saying this because too much goes unsaid. A writer talks about the world in edited versions; redacted for public consumption. And yet there are little moments of shame and anxiety that never get spoken. They remain unsaid for all our lives. People die with heaps of things unsaid; things of tenderness and of love, or things that are just too shameful to admit. What the therapists call 'baggage', as they offer themselves to be the one with whom we can unburden.

But I'm taking a different road. I'm choosing you and maybe others I have loved.

My penis wasn't mine for a week but maybe penis is the wrong word. This is about the phallus; a mythic dimension of being here which constitutes masculinity. Associated in the deep recesses of our consciousness with sexual prowess, the glory of being loved, the heat of passion, the fire of ecstasy. It's all embodied in the word 'phallus', and the word itself is embodied in the person; every man's secret is related to this embodiment.

But it is also a delusion, and it all becomes intensely comic when men age and lose their grip on this embodied meaning. When the wash of years across the bow leaves them rudderless. When high blood pressure, or lazy hearts, or exhaustion from excessive self-reflection leaves them limp and lifeless. Then they are endured only as clowns. And there's fuck all left of the divine phallus once you stick a rubber hose pipe into a man's bladder. Any memory of potency, masculinity or sexual pleasure is wiped from history.

I was surrendered to another sense of self; a broken self was opened, like a new space, a new floor, a new ground to carry the heft of my consciousness. Of course, I hoped it would only be for one night. But the doctor refused to say exactly how long this impalement might last. The following morning in the busy ward half a dozen young men and women in white coats holding clipboards assembled around the towering presence of a consultant who glowed and sparkled like a new baby freshly soaped and scrubbed, behind his yellow dickie bow.

A young doctor asked if I consented to him having a look.

'Yes, of course,' I said, because when we are vulnerable, we make extra efforts to please our masters, and so the sheets were pulled back.

'The skin is chafed', the young doctor concluded, as if I had failed.

'Correct,' the big man said. 'And why?'

The young man didn't know. I think he lost some brownie points.

The big man ignored him, as he covered me again with the sheets. 'We will get the nurse to give you something for that,' he said.

I thanked him. 'It's sore,' I declared, having lost all shame.

'Of course it is,' he agreed. As if 'sore' was as obvious as saying the sky was blue. 'We can see how you're getting on after a week.'

He looked triumphant with this conclusion.

I was miserable.

'And you're doing fine,' he said, before they all left. 'We'll see you tomorrow.'

They pulled the curtains fully open as they left, and I wished they had just left them closed so that I did not have to stare at people in other beds. So that they would not stare at me, and at the tube running from between my legs down onto the floor and into a bag of amber liquid.

One or two days might have been okay but a week was too long. Hard to move in bed at night and hard to get out. And the nurses came and went, with laxatives and bedpans. Occasionally I walked up and down with the bag in my hand. I sat out in a chair. I lay depressed until a nurse spoke my name loudly and insisted I get out. The bag was clipped to a small plastic stand beside the bed, and occasionally it fell over and the hose tugged in my groin suddenly and the nurse would rush to examine it and make sure it had not become dislodged. At night the bag filled up and a nurse came with a dish and opened the spout at the bottom of the bag so that the liquid poured out. I listened, as urine emptied from the bag in a comic splutter, and then a great flood. I apologised to her for the smell.

'That's no problem,' she said, smiling. 'It's our job.'

I resigned myself to a clown's life.

How could I have been so blithe in commending my mother to a nursing home all those years ago? How could I have been so glib over the years about friends and relations who fell seriously ill, endured long weeks in hospitals, before their last day? How could I not have understood that in hospital every small moment is a catastrophe for the ego? Until you are discharged. Set free again.

It was a nurse called Anita who came on that last day in Beaumont. I remember her name; she came with rubber gloves and a silver dish and other accoutrements on a trolley.

I thought it was going to be an elaborate procedure. But she just yanked it out with a flick of her wrist.

The rubber hose was gone. My bladder felt free.

I thanked her because it was just a small act of kindness, and one more small miracle of hospital life.

'You're free to go,' she said, smiling, 'once we get your meds and a letter from the doctors.'

I wished her a happy Easter. I walked free and cured, and I had forgotten about you and all that I had planned to tell you, by the time I reached home.

It's too late now to be sensitive. I've lived my life with almost callous indifference to the wounded and the broken. I've been glib beyond belief about the enormity of human suffering. And it was only when I found myself in the thick of it, on the slab of the operating theatre, in the bed with cot sides, and a remote control for lowering and raising my body, that I woke up. It was only when I had to face this small discomfort, this tube in the bladder for a short week, only then did I discover how terrible it is to lose one's lovely heroic sense of self. To embrace the comic phallus.

The body is in decay and destined for death and the journey is about surrendering not just to the truth of it, but to the others who turn up to take care of you and take control of you. And that's why I fled to the ocean. That's why I came here to be alone, week after week and month after month. Why was I so afraid to let go? Probably for the same reason that I never wrote letters.

The year had passed simply enough with nothing but the sound of the sea, the wild Atlantic, and the screens of my laptop, desktop and phone, and the names of old friends that I yearned for and wanted so desperately to communicate with. I had a microphone for podcasting but not all the talking or writing in the world could heal me. Because a writer can talk until the cows come home to a plurality of people and perhaps never speak intimately or spontaneously, one to one.

It's hard to believe that any writer would live so cautiously, but the impediment afflicts many. The affectation of public intimacy on a stage or in a book is often linked with that inability to be emotionally spontaneous on a one-to-one level. And emails can be a remedy for this problem in a writer's life.

Although my emails have always been as cold as steel.

Perhaps it was the send button on the computer that blocked me from being personal with anyone apart from one old school friend. And it struck me that if I wrote with a pen and paper I might find more courage.

So I began writing in the morning. It was a ritual. Then I'd go walking on the beach. Then sometimes return and finish it off. And as I walked the beach it was always shame or remorse that drove me to go back to the desk and write more and more.

But of course, nothing got posted.

I would begin a letter in the early evening, and as the nights got longer and the days shortened, I found myself by the light of a lamp, with my image in the glass of the window before me. That usually ended my reveries with the dead and the long forgotten and the people who dream of afterlives and spirit worlds. I would close the curtains and put on the light, and then the television, and watch Netflix, and assure myself that I had returned to some more real world.

At Christmas I was with my beloved, though the quiet and collective worry about the Covid disease enfolded us all in a kind of uneasy restraint. Until the days lengthened again and another springtime arrived and still I stood at the cliff and looked into the ocean and wrote my little confessions and wondered why.

And here I am at the end of summer 2022. The wind in my face. The sand beneath my feet. Prospero with his microphones and amplifiers, I sit staring at my microphone making podcasts.

I remember a story about a Russian cosmonaut who used to circle Earth alone in his little ship, and for company he found a man in Donegal on the edge of the ocean and they would talk to each other on radio waves, surfing words up and down, from Earth to space and back again. I feel like that cosmonaut, podcasting to unknown listeners, invisible ones who sit with me once a week as I speak into their ears. Ears I never see or touch. I am Prospero with his microphones, and the waves hurt my eyes and the sun is shining in the window. I am Hamlet talking to himself.

When I was a young man loitering around the mineral bar at dances in Glangevlin Hall, in the mountains of west Cavan, I wore a long grey army coat that I had bought from an Oxfam shop. An old army coat. It was a fashion back then and I might have thought of myself as the lonely poet wrapped in his own melancholy, but in truth I was always looking for a mother; for a woman who would reach me in places my own mother never went. Spaces of tenderness in me yearned to be opened.

And never were.

I put another letter in the waste basket and threw a big weather-proof cape over me and headed for the wild headlands to hear the ocean's roar. That's the danger with writing letters. One minute you are shaping words of kindness to another human being and then all of a sudden the words explode on the page and your unconscious shatters and you see something clearly that you never saw before.

I was only looking for Mother. No wonder I lay on the hospital pillow with an open hand, fantasising about someone holding it.

I didn't know myself. That's why, until this past year, letters never got written. Because letters don't just reveal us to the reader. They reveal the author.

The me is exposed to myself in a letter. The process is as well refined as therapy. Isn't that what they did in the nineteenth century, sitting for so long at their Pembroke tables and their Davenport desks, writing epistles day after day to their sisters and mothers or their brothers on the battlefields?

To a Writer

Dermot Healy was an Irish writer of enormous stature, who died in June 2014, a Zen master who hid himself in a forest of words, and fashioned beautiful books and poems and lived on the edge of the Atlantic in Sligo with his beloved.

Dermot,

It is the beginning of May 2021 and nearing the anniversary of your death; I knew you since I was 16, when I went knocking on your door in search of guidance. Teach me how to be a writer, I pleaded. And you taught me, that and much more besides, before we drifted apart.

Sometimes it's as if you are on the beach with me. Walking as we did one summer in the '80s, when you were in Matthew Sweeney's mother's cottage in Donegal and I stayed overnight and sang your praises as the best writer I had read since O'Flaherty.

'You carry the sacramental depth of things in your stories,'

I declared. 'You bring animals into your writing like no other writer has done since O'Flaherty.'

And there are times I still wake in the morning to see the sun coming in the window, as if you were still in the world and about to surprise me with a cup of tea as you did on that morning long ago in Donegal, or even earlier, in '75, when I stayed over with you and Anne Marie near Killykeen and you joked that you'd write me into your book.

We promised each other the world. And it feels like yesterday and yet so many years have passed since I walked the beach on the day I heard of your death.

I suppose there is always someone who goes first. And as my beard turns white, just like yours, I look around the room thinking of all our contemporaries and wonder who will be next.

We slip from youth to achievements, and we think ourselves the most gifted in the universe.

No time was ever as good as our time. No place mattered like our place matters. But to be fully human is to waken to the slip and slide of things, and to notice the world and all its glory drift away into the distance. The prizes, the readings, the lecture tours, and the adulation of reviewers and critics and audiences all evaporates. Folds itself like a mist that moves along the beach in a tumbleweed of air.

Or to put it another way, the ice beneath our feet is thin. On a lake the ice cracks and you look out from where you stand close to the shoreline and you see someone slip down. They were far out, so their slipping away is natural.

Every death is like this; like watching a drowning on a lake on which you are already walking. They are walking out there and in an instant their world cracks and they fall out of sight. But it doesn't bother you because you're near the shoreline.

Then one morning the sun draws you. And you are not afraid because there are others, around you, with you, all walking in the same direction. All going deeper and deeper out onto the lake. And you walk out believing in yourself, like you might be Jesus. And the ice glistens. And even when someone up ahead slips and you hear the ice crack and witness them go into the dark it doesn't bother you. You are closer now but you are brave.

You travel further to the centre of the lake until there is no one ahead of you and you feel fragile on the ice. Your feet can feel it. You are vulnerable. Then suddenly someone beside you falls through the cracking sheets of frost and the loss brings you closer to the moment of your own destiny.

Like ice, your little world will break and fall asunder, and you will slip down to oblivion. That's how I felt when you died. When you slipped into the dark I was in Donegal. We had just rented a lovely little summer house for the weekend. It even had a hot tub on the patio. Not that we needed a hot tub, because we were surrounded by the ocean.

I have come to love this ocean from every angle. Especially from the window of the plane that takes me to and from Dublin. There is no airport with as exquisite an approach: the white waves, black rocks, and deep blue of the ocean rolling in and out, and the glistening sand dunes as the aircraft banks, dips, drops, lands out of the blue sky onto the apron beside the beach.

Or alternatively going up into the air as the plane reaches 20, 30, 50 feet and the waves and swimmers shrink until the coast is like a Google map. I can take it all in like someone who has already left the human sphere and is looking back.

That's when I feel you beside me in the next seat. You are a ghost and I ask you, 'Will death be like this, Dermot? Tell me because you must know now. Unless there is nothing left of you.'

At least your death wasn't a lonely experience, according to reports I heard from people who were there. Yourself and the neighbours, celebrating something small and private in the living room of that cottage on the lip of the ocean, the crest of the cliff, where you established yourself and Helen as king and queen of each other's hearts; the howling windy world where you began to look like Ezra Pound in photographs and talked to the geese that flew across from Canada to call you home.

Yes, I know you had a special love for Canada, and that you travelled there with Helen when your masterful novel *A Goat's Song* became a hit.

But who could tell that your little private celebration on that day would become so public. Who could imagine the drama that was about to play out as you and Helen and your neighbours raised your glasses to toast each other; that in minutes you would be on the floor, having lost consciousness, as a neighbour woman, a nurse, leaned over the body and tried to resuscitate the great poet. Who could imagine that while the food in the kitchen was still warm, they would end the afternoon picking over and over the sudden facts and trying to piece together what happened, and shape an image to share with the world. They tried to make words that might convey the terror if it. A notice for the newspapers. Dermot Healy died suddenly this afternoon.

A tree had fallen.

A light had gone out.

The world was smaller.

There were so many different ways to say it. Not that it matters to you now. From that moment there was no going back. No more possibility to embody sweet moments of love or tenderness. They were all over. The ice had broken beneath you and you were gone.

And you were the one closest to me on the ice. And life could never be the same without you.

But your death was only the first of many. Suddenly and dramatically, dying in your beloved's arms, beneath the beating palms of a nurse's hands trying to revive your failed heart.

On 22 May I returned to Machaire Uí Rabhartaigh, where the hot tub had once stood on the decking of a cottage for rent. But it was all closed now. The day was wild and windy on the sea and the fragile ferry from Toraigh Island got battered from all sides as it made its way through the waves.

Scread na Bealtaine they called it. Or another phrase I heard them use was 'Bealtaine's revenge on the cuckoo'.

It comes for three days, stirs up the seas and so the

lobster pots will be full because the *gliomaigh* do be stirred. But don't put your pots out during the storm. It's the week after that things will be good.

And remember that if a small storm comes at the beginning of May, there will surely be a second one later.

So the fisherfolk said.

I was on the deck beside the hot tub in 2014, wondering why anyone would want a hot tub by the ocean, and worrying that the clouds over Errigal did not augur well for the following day, when the phone rang. It was a journalist from RTÉ. They wanted me to say something on the following morning's news show. I did.

Mumbling the kind of rhetoric that people do when a great writer has passed. Eulogising you in sonorous terms. Your likes would not be seen again, I said.

My private sorrow was that I had not seen much of you in decades. It was the same remorse I had felt when John O'Donohue died. I had neglected our friendship. And if friendship is not nourished, it dies. Now it was too late to ever walk the strand with you again as I did that long-ago time in Donegal when you were in the middle of a last draft and you sent me a copy and then invited me up to discuss it.

We walked on that strand with hangovers and I tried to tell you I loved you. Instead I sang the praises of the book. How the sacramental depth of nature manifests in your sentences, just like Kavanagh. When all I really wanted to say was that I loved you from when I first heard your voice in the little café your mother and aunt ran in Cavan town, and when you liberated me from the mundane language of a middle-class childhood by subverting every word you used. It wasn't just your voice I loved. Your smiling eyes. Your self-mockery. All those things are how we name our love for someone.

But with you it was like a brother. Though my mother thought you a rogue, you always claimed her, greeting her on the street with your seductive eyes so that later she would say, 'I met Dermot in town today; he's not bad really.' And when I went to the café your mother would always take me by the hand and lead me to the stairs and say, 'He's still in the bed reading; go up and call him down and I'll put on breakfast for both of you.' The entire world seemed to love you because you were so unique. And you could give everyone the feeling that you had come into the world just for them.

That's how I felt. That you were there for me. You had come into the world to meet me. I had come into the world to meet you. That in previous lives we had known each other for thousands of years.

Sometimes when you were drunk you would take a mouthful of whiskey and then embrace someone with a kiss, the whiskey on your lips surprising them. Such public displays of intimacy were common back then as people lost themselves in the smoky bars of rural Ireland, and I longed for some such intimacy that might be a language to express my feelings.

I was 17. And you were 24. I was not certain then in what way I might master the language of desire, or how I might negotiate my way towards love. I saw your companions glow in the intimacy of a shared language with you; a physical bond. And all I could muster was the critic's drum, saying things because I could not say anything else. Saying that I read 'The Cow's Death' by Liam O'Flaherty and noting how deep was the sense of presence in his animals. How they felt pain and joy. And how an animal's emotions were as clear as a human being's. 'Was this a literary trick?' I asked, to make the animals psychologically human.

And I answered my own question.

'No,' I said. 'There is something deeper in O'Flaherty. A revelation of emotion in the animal in a way that touches us because we cannot rise to the raw level of such feeling.'

Or at least I couldn't. And when my dissertation was over, you turned to the woman beside you and her lips met yours and she laughed with joy and surprise to feel the whiskey stinging her tongue.

Perhaps it's why we went our separate ways. Although to be truthful there were other reasons. Your soul remembered some karmic trauma. You carried what you called the hurt mind, the consciousness formed and shaped in fire and agony somewhere long ago, and as you struggled with it, and fought with shadows of your own making, so the people close to you endured it. They endured you and needed enormous courage and strength to stand with you, and sometimes to stand up to you. They had to negotiate complex pathways, to avoid the withering of their own dreams, because of the attention that you demanded.

But I didn't know much of those struggles with demons. I knew you as a boy. As a startled fawn, a wondering, joyful deer that is surprised by its own life, and the sacramental presence that filters through it. It was long before drink took hold and long before those remembered agonies and traumas ripened into shadows all around you. You were to me the great poet, lover, joyful priest of love. And I didn't want to lie with you because my proclivity was not at any deep level driven by sexual longing. But your capacity for intimacy with other souls left me always empty, like a lover is empty when they see their champion pass whispers from their lips to a stranger.

I remember fingering your book in Derrylin, at the kitchen table, feeling that I was living a moment of history. I was reading a book that would be remembered. That kind of reverence for you was something I retained for many years even though we had grown apart.

Goodbye to the sweetshop in Cavan. Farewell to the afternoons in Grogan's, I said.

As we grew old our lives were distilled into separate narratives as is often the case with childhood friends. We became more isolated. More solitary creatures. And we read each other from a distance and remained in love.

No wonder I felt such grief and sorrow at your death.

About all the dead I felt the same remorse, for not being more attentive to them when they were alive. And remorse too that those they left behind had slipped my mind. That all the good intentions I had of writing to this or that grieving, broken-hearted partner was all talk and all intention, and yet never acted on.

And even among the living there were people I could yet write to. My remorse wasn't grief. It was self-indulgence. I was even silent in the face of living souls, loved ones, and perhaps even some or all of my old enemies whom I could have written to, if I really cared.

But instead I walked the sandy beaches during May, thinking about you. And thinking about a line from Rumi.

There is a field; I will meet you there.

What did that mean? I just walked and walked and stood on a headland and listened to the waves because I did not know. And then I forgot you again.

So that's the pattern. I think of you. Then I write to someone else. Then I walk the beach. And then I think of you again. And I can name the others. But how can I name you? You are so precious, so special, so wonderful.

JUNE 2021

Of course I missed my own beloved. Although I saw her at weekends, I was creating a private life on the beach for myself. It was like an affair with the sky. And I was happier to be alone with my physical problems. I still could not function in the bathroom without a variety of medicines. The struggle to waken the gut constituted a good portion of every day. On the beach my legs sang out as if they had been drenched in a bed of nettles, despite three painkillers a day to still the damaged nerves there and in my back.

Like a sore cat that hides under the stairs or in the remotest part of the loft after being battered by a car, I needed to be alone to heal physically and come to terms with the extent to which my body was not functioning normally.

Yes I missed her, but I suppose that's another aspect of illness; it's like another country, and there are places where you can only go alone.

Every morning I get an urge to write more letters. The names of old friends come into my mind. Even old enemies. People I knew for decades, and some I'd met for only a few moments or a few days and yet their presence had a lasting effect on me. Some that I just long for with unresolved attachment that lasts for decades.

It's amazing how the desire for another person can sustain decades of their absence. Or else I forget about them until I uncover a letter or a Christmas card, folded into the leaves of an old bible or novel, and all of a sudden they are in the room again and everything I once felt for them, longing and desire and unrestrained admiration, rises like a tornado.

So when I sit at the Pembroke table and open the drawer and take out an envelope and a few sheets of A4 paper I always end up writing to someone else.

With some letters I don't get beyond staring at the blank page. With others I manage to gather a few paragraphs on the page before lumping it into a ball and tossing it into the waste basket.

And then there are letters I finish. Because I pour my heart into them. I sign off and lick the back of an envelope and stamp it. I feel delighted. Liberated. The stamp seals the intention. As if €1.10 was an enormous price for a stamp and by virtue of sticking it to the envelope, I had completed the task.

But not even one gets posted. They lie in the dainty drawer that slides in and out of my beautiful Pembroke table.

The table, like everything else in my life, was an accident.

It happened in Bundoran. It was meant for another customer but when the other fellow saw the black stripes along the legs, and realised that they were inlaid as a mark of remembrance for Admiral Nelson, he wasn't impressed. I don't know what he had against Nelson but the table remained unloved before my eyes and the auctioneer explained that the original of the species was designed by Lord Pembroke for his wife who was a distinguished writer in the eighteenth century. It contained two drop-leaf sides and a drawer in which there was a neat writing unit; a lid rolled with leather and various compartments within for envelopes, sheets of paper and even ink. Dark-blue ink stained the interior of the drawer, from which I could sense the presence of some letter-writing lady who might have just left the room. Imagining a rustling dress, I felt the wonders and pleasures of writing a letter at that desk might be enormous, and as a writer I could resist it no longer.

'I will write letters at this table,' I told the auctioneer.

He stared at me. 'Michael,' he said, 'this table doesn't belong to you. You're only the caretaker of it for a while. And if it survived 200 years without being damaged, it is a pity that it would be battered on your watch.'

So when I fled to Donegal I began again, because I thought the Pembroke was most suitable for writing letters. And now, each morning it is this table that calls me to write. I use a Parker pen that was gifted to me in lieu of payment for a workshop. And I write the address and the name on the envelope before I begin. Afterwards the envelope is consigned to the largest compartment in the table drawer. Along with all the others.

To an Old School Friend

No more texts and emails. I'm writing this to you with a new pen. I'd like to update you on the situation here at the beach. I'm improved a lot since March and the dark days of the catheter. I know I've gone on a lot about the hospital, but I am grateful as well. It's almost two months since I got out of Beaumont, and I can walk almost 3,000 steps on a good morning, although I take painkillers to assuage the nerve damage to my colon, guts and legs. Sometimes the feet get so hot I think they're burning. I touch them and they are as cold as marble.

I'm trying to have a normal life here. For example I was in Bundoran last week. I dropped into my friend Vincent in the antique shop where I first saw the Pembroke table. This time I couldn't resist it. The other one is in Leitrim, that gorgeous little writing desk with a lid finished in red leather. Vincent reminded me of it.

'You don't need another table for writing,' he said. 'You have a Davenport desk!'

Apparently it was made originally for some sea captain who wanted something neat for the ocean, and dainty so that it could be moved around the captain's tiny cabin. I told Vincent that it was in Leitrim and that I was heading to the coast to recuperate and be alone, and he just turned his eyes to heaven.

'I'm taking money off you,' he said, 'and I might as well be taking it off a child.'

But it cried out to me from the corner. How elegant it would be by the sea to write letters from it with such a dainty drawer for writing materials and even an inkwell, all hidden away beneath the lid finished with green leather.

'Vincent,' I pleaded, 'that table is crying out to me. It's like a relic of Mister Darcy and Elizabeth Bennet's love for each other; it's like my entire childhood imagination all rolled into one beautiful surface. Give it to me. Please.'

I couldn't leave the shop without it.

'Okay, okay, okay, I suppose you'll not regret it,' Vincent said. 'Sure we're only custodians of these things. And it's a beautiful object.'

He delivered it and we placed it under the window in my office and here I am. I'm sitting at it with this pen and just enjoying the silence of the house. I can hear the clock ticking in the hallway and a slight whine through one of the kitchen windows where the breeze comes in. And I hear the sound of an occasional car very far away. Other than those interruptions I'm absorbed by a great ocean of silence and the desk is my compass, my anchor, my stepping stone.

But my words tapered off when I tried to describe the negative side of all this.

There was a beautiful silence on the beach. But in the house sometimes the silence was dark and daunting; maybe even intimidating.

As if the entire ocean outside had created its own negative inside the house. Or perhaps it was just inside me.

The silence was empty but as large as the ocean. And though all the tables in my life were like stepping-stones I never used, or like an unrelenting call to wake and reach out to the other people around me before it was too late, and though the illness had frightened me to the stark fact that soon enough it would be too late, yet I couldn't begin this letter. I couldn't get started. I couldn't write. And in the past letters didn't get written because they contained things that are best left unsaid.

Some say that the importance of speaking the truth is over-rated. And yet in ancient times people would often tell their secrets to the bees. Perhaps because the bees don't tell anyone else. Perhaps because to tell it to the bees was some kind of release. And many say that in the telling of things we find peace and forgiveness. And sometimes I felt that the silent house was full of ghosts sitting in the corners, around the table in the kitchen, or on benches in the hallway, waiting for me to speak.

It was an image that came out of a dream my beloved had the night before I left for Donegal.

She dreamed of men, perhaps a dozen or so, all coming into the house and sitting down and waiting.

And I thought I knew what they were waiting for. They wanted me to speak. And out in the garden during June there were bees everywhere on the fuchsia, or buzzing around the escallonia.

Why would they do that? The fuchsia was not yet in flower. Neither was the escallonia. And the answer I gave myself was that they were waiting for me to talk.

To tell them my secrets.

To say something.

I had things I needed to say because I feared that

I would become ill if I kept them bottled up. And yet they were the things that can't be said to anyone.

So who could I turn to? And what could possibly make me better? I had the ocean to speak with, but it wasn't enough.

I want to write letters. But it always ends up the same. As if the bees were calling me to talk, the dead were calling me to pay attention, and the walls of the house were calling me to prayer.

Is this what it feels like to be ill? I wondered. Or is this how it feels when you have taken the path of healing?

Just a quick note. It is almost the end of June. At night my legs are still singing in pain and I still can't go to the bathroom without taking high doses of laxative. I can't walk the beach without anxiety. I can't function socially. Maybe ill health grows out of secrets. Maybe there is worse to come if I don't open up.

Write it down. Tell someone. Anyone. Maybe you.

But I tore it up and tossed it in the waste basket.

To a Lover

It's not as firm a world as we think, and as I get older I thought I would miss you less. 1984 is a long time ago. You receded into the background, into a fog of memory. After all, I met my beloved and we have had a wonderful life and you are hidden somewhere further back in my past. In my youth.

But that's the problem.

I wake as an old man. From being there with you to being here now, I wake terribly alone at this beach because the days that were between us, the moments of half-smoked cigarettes, are gone.

The wave breaks.

There is nothing of you left.

Perhaps the next person you met was the right one for you. The next person I met was certainly the right one for me. We were blessed with happiness. It's like floating on the ocean. But yet sometimes I wake and it is yesterday again. And the terrible anguish of ageing is that we cannot forget our youth.

An old woman I know has just passed away. She was happy all her life, loyal to a strong man who fought in a war, and she was proud of him and would smile and glow at the dinner table when he was asked about driving a tank and about all he saw and did. And she worked in her garden and was robust in the kitchen and she hung garlic on the rafters and dried flowers from the ceiling.

She was mother and grandmother to a great tribe of warriors but then in Covid she found herself in a nursing home. Well, we all end up in a nursing home, you might say, if we are lucky.

But she ended up in the wrong nursing home. One she didn't like. And there was no way out, and Covid made a prisoner of her, and she grew angry so that when they spoke to her on the screens it wasn't a picture of serenity they saw, or something the news bulletins could weave a feel-good sentimental narrative around, but an angry woman raging with the world for caging her like a dog.

And yes, the truth is she was caged like a dog, and then she died. She was one of the many who died during the pandemic. There was no happy ending, there was no inquest, there was no one held to account.

Her life fades now. She is forgotten and even her family

who loved her have two problems. They don't know why she got so angry and they don't know how to remember her.

So forgetfulness comes for different reasons.

We forget what we don't like.

And she was forgotten, like so much more.

Is that what worries me most about you and I? That I should one day wake in a nursing home and have forgotten our love, our dancing, our late nights, our skin-on-skin eyeballing each other with the shock of what might come next?

Is that what worries me? Or is it the prospect that your memory would actually haunt me and disturb me and I would want to banish you from my mind entirely?

I saw two bees on the beach one day in the same flower, a purple harebell, and I looked in and they were entwined in each other's limbs and I thought of you. It was like what we did on those afternoons in the heat. The best time for lovemaking, as Ovid used to say.

To sleep with someone else is to know you are not alone. To sleep with the beloved is to fall unconscious in the embrace of the other. To let go of your own consciousness in surrender to the one who is awake. And it's something that rarely happens with lovers. They meet and kiss and make love and then turn their backs to each other on the pillow and dream silently and secretly away from each other.

But not us.

I suppose it was Rumi that conjured your ghost up for me again. Your skin gone brown in the heat on those nights we leaned in on the single candle in the room, and I told you about the moths that Rumi talked of. Although I didn't have the story right.

A moth goes to the flame, I said. A moth goes towards the flame. He says to the other moths, behold that light yonder. I wonder what it is. It flickers over there in the corner. I shall go and examine it. So he goes and then he comes back and he says that light is very, very bright. So the second moth goes over and he comes back and he says it's not just bright but it's very, very hot as well when you get close to it. And then the third says this is interesting. I too shall go and examine this wonderful light. And so he goes over but he never returns.

Do you remember that? I told it and you laughed and said you didn't know what it was about and you interrogated me about each moth:

What kind of personalities they might have had?

Why were they so curious?

Why could they not just get on with their lives?

You wouldn't take the story seriously. But the next day Luigi, our landlord, came to the door and he had a basket of fruit from the garden and you took the fruit and said, 'Hey, Luigi, come in, come in.'

And he came in, still wearing his linen white jacket over his shoulders like he always did, and sunglasses hiding the sorrow in his eyes, and a little white hat making him appear like a gangster in the mafia.

You told him the story and even though his English wasn't so great, he got it. I could see, even behind the shaded glass, that he was weeping. And it was because you told it so well. So beautifully.

You told it like you understood it. No; you told it like it was your story. Like something in you had created the story and it was your story now.

And as Luigi's eyes watered you asked him why he was so sad, and he went to the door and beckoned us to follow, and we went out and followed him to a swing seat beneath a majestic weeping willow.

He pointed at the garden and he said, 'All this was for me and my wife. We made this. It was our Paradiso. But when we had it finished, she went away. She went to the light. And never returned. It is still Paradiso. But she is gone. Like the moth. She never came back.'

He knew that the light was to the moth as the presence of God is for human beings. That we are attracted to it and go towards it until eventually it burns us up. And he knew that the way we get burned is by illness, old age, and the deterioration of the body. But he also knew that these things are only sent to us as forms of light, and that the light is obscure, enveloped in darkness. It seems as if the darkness enfolds us but in fact we are simply moving closer and closer to the light.

That's what Luigi took from the story. And that's what you knew, because if you didn't then you would not have been able to tell it so eloquently.

And I knew that there would be no more lovemaking that afternoon. That your heart had been taken by another. Even though we were in our twenties and Luigi may have been in his fifties, or older, his sorrow had swallowed you, and I would have to leave you alone for some hours.

What is there left, now? Just this ageing and raging and the bittersweet memory of times that were eternal and yet are gone?

And the age that creeps up my hands and arms, and appears in my eyes? Because I wear sunglasses now just like Luigi did.

A light that will burn me up sometime soon.

Enough said, my love. I will go walking on the beach.

By the end of June I was melancholic. I woke early, despite the heavy curtains, and I walked the beach, pondering all the people I had failed to tell how much I loved them or appreciated them or was sorry that I had offended them. My address book was a litany of failure. Old friends to whom I could have sent messages of love or hope while there was still time.

I made porridge every morning because even though the weather was improving, I had been told that porridge was good for the gut and the digestive system, and that it would contribute to a healthy body. I lived in hope.

But then one wet Saturday I burned the porridge on the range, because I was looking out the window so long, I forgot about it. I was naming people I regretted not writing to. A truck driver who gave me a lift to Italy; him and me and John O'Donohue at the top of the Alps in 1981, sharing stories in the cabin of a truck with a naggin of whiskey before descending the zig-zag narrow drive into Italy the following morning. I meant to write to that truck driver for years; until one morning a friend phoned me to say he had died, homeless on the streets of Liverpool.

That night in the Alps I sensed that he belonged nowhere. That the endless road across Europe in his truck was a metaphor for his heart's long search for home. And I should have written to him about that. But I didn't. And then it was too late.

And there was a student in Maynooth with whom I had a difference of opinion, a small argument, but we never healed it. And years later I bought a postcard with an image of two monks on it. One had his arm on the shoulder of the other fellow and the caption on the card read 'Friendship'.

But I never posted it. He died suddenly in his early fifties. And when I heard the news, I was standing in my office, the phone at my ear, and the postcard sitting on the shelf beside me.

And a storm came, just like the one at the beginning of the month, and the windows rattled all night and the blinds flapped like sails and I thought I imagined men from my beloved's dreams.

She had dreamed of old-fashioned men sitting around in this Donegal house the night before we bought it.

They were waiting for her.

And now I was alone, and I could feel them close to me. A benevolent and collective presence in the storm's effect on the house, on the creaking doors, the floorboards, and the rafters overhead.

In the morning I looked in the mirror and realised that I too was wearing clothes that matched the style of old men long ago.

Black trousers, a waistcoat and a black linen jacket.

It was the only time I ever got into bed in the middle of the day in many years. I stripped and was under the blankets when a knock came upon the door. The only knock upon the door that ever happened since I had arrived in the house.

So I lay still, and slightly fearful that whoever was there might come around the back and look in the window. But it was only the postman.

By the time I had dressed and opened the door I could see his van moving off from a neighbour's house further down the road. I tried to wave him down but he didn't see me.

Later I went to the post office and inquired for the parcel.

'The postman is not back yet,' she said, 'but he will try your door again tomorrow.'

The following day I waited in the kitchen, dressed in the same black waistcoat and jacket, with a clean white shirt, until he arrived and handed me the box. I opened it and took out a gold pocket watch on a chain, which I attached to a buttonhole, and I slipped the watch into the waistcoat pocket.

And yes, I went out to the town wearing the black clothes and a flat cap like some old folksy man, with my belly protruding and the golden chain dangling from between the breast pocket and the buttonhole. I checked the image in the glass door of SuperValu. It was complete. I had arrived. But it was fair to say that I was alone.

Then one morning, early enough for the beach to feel timeless, I was back again at Machaire Uí Rabhartaigh, and the sea was so calm that it reminded me of Rosses Point on Sligo Bay. There is a silence in both places which is substantial, between one limpid wave and the next. Each tiny splash falling into silence and then from that silence the next little splash arrives. The distance between one wave and another is like the space between musical notes. It's the space where you really listen.

And I remember going out to Rosses Point regularly with Mary McPartlan, when I lived in Sligo. She and I would walk along the beach at that same hour, after dawn, and the same waves would fall on the strand as do in Machaire Uí Rabhartaigh and the same silences would rise between the waves, and the past and the present became so fused on that Donegal beach that I felt I was walking again with Mary, on another beach and in another time. When I returned to the house I sat at the desk and wrote this note.

To a Singer

Mary McPartlan was a lecturer at University College Galway, a Fulbright scholar and a gifted musician and singer. Her contribution to Irish culture, education and music was enormous and her death in April of 2020 was the cause of terrible grief compounded by restrictions in force during the Covid lockdown.

Mary,

Do you remember singing 'A Rainy Night in Soho' at a concert in Westmeath eight years ago? It's not a long time. It was in a church and I wrote about it later in a column and you phoned me up to thank me. It's still true. The angels in the decorated windows looked sad, and I was thinking that maybe they would come down from their cold eternity of stained glass and join in the craic. And then your eyes met mine.

The song is a beautiful declaration of love.

It was just a coincidence, but it summed up our love. We were like brother and sister. And I sometimes felt that the love of your family, and your own brothers and sisters, was the real heartbeat in your life. And when you reached out to others, like me or Vincent Woods or all the great musicians that you gathered together like a mother hen beneath your wings, it was as if they became extensions of your family love. Loving you always meant belonging to a family. That's what people were missing and that's what you gave with such generosity.

I remember when you used to sing on the sofa in 17, The Mall. You and Mary Gilhooly from Drumkeeran. Mary's flat was on the second floor and I was renting the flat on the third floor in the same building and your voice came to me, up through the floorboards, and I went down and opened the door to see your face.

I've been listening to you a long time, Mary. Ever since that first evening in 1975.

You were singing 'The Galway Shawl', a popular ballad of the time, and then suddenly you turned into Ewan MacColl's beautiful love song 'The First Time Ever I Saw Your Face'.

I always wondered was it me coming into the room that made you change gear in that moment. We had a habit back then of speaking our hearts in the lyrics of songs. After all, I was only 22 and you were 21.

I saw you in the big tent at the Ballisodare Folk Festival, and Paul Brady came over to you afterwards to say hello. I think that was August of 1977. Forty-five years ago.

My goodness, you travelled far since then, Mary.

Do you remember the prayer meetings I used to attend on a Thursday night in Sligo? And you'd walk down the street with me, because you were off to your Connolly Youth meetings. And afterwards we'd link up in the Trades Club. Singing love songs all night. You could raise your voice for Joe Hill, and Mandela, and the refugee camps in Lebanon. And you had a song for everyone, and your voice silenced the little circle of heroes that would gather in the Trades Club, bare-boarded, with forums to sit on, and Packie Duignan would bow his head and rest his flute on his knees to take in the draught of your meaning, the sweetness of your voice, and the power of your poetic folk songs.

Imagine, Duignan, famous and brilliant on his instrument, a master musician, raising his hand and calling for quiet so that you would be heard.

'*Ciúnas*,' Máirtín Enright, the sweet Kerry singer, would call.

My goodness, Mary, those were nights, as Rumi says, when we found the wine that was ready before the grapes were grown. Those were the nights when I saw in your face the face you had before you were born.

And it's been a long and winding road since then, and you went your way and found your beloved, and I went off on my adventures as a priest, and yet that brotherly and sisterly affection and intimacy we had back then always remained.

When I saw you in a car park in Galway, 40 years later, across the roofs of a hundred vehicles, I saw a sister.

And I loved you.

And I suppose in the decades towards the end of your life I never said that clearly.

I regret it, Mary, because your heart was a field beyond what was right or wrong. Your heart was a field where grew the thorn and the rose, the thistle and the wild mountain thyme.

And wherever you are this morning, Mary, as I pen these words looking out on the Atlantic, I imagine your heart as a field of sunflowers.

Rumi says that whoever brought us here will take us home. But we didn't think you'd leave so soon.

It's as if you dissolved into the night behind the stained glass window. 'Whoever brought us here will take us home' was my prayer this morning, as I walked the beach, feeling the wind in my hair and on my cheeks. Feeling the sound of it in my ears and knowing how lucky I am.

I'm still here.

No more to be said.

Whoever brought me here will take me home too, eventually.

Sometimes an old-fashioned writing desk or an antique bureau allows me to affect a kind of Victorian sincerity, a kind of George Eliot clarity.

'My dear friend,' I begin. As if I were Edward Casaubon in *Middlemarch* waiting all morning for rain and thought I might idle the time at the writing desk.

But there are other letters which frighten me because I don't know before I begin what's going to come out. And then it spills. And I read back and wonder about all the emotions that were bottled inside me. Or perhaps the emotions just flare up the more I write, like the ocean churning up more and more foam when it's angry.

One way or another, I couldn't send a letter to Mary.

She had died in April 2020, during the first Covid lockdown when almost nobody could attend her funeral, or even visit her in hospital as she lay dying. And even when I was in Donegal that summer, with a sore leg, wondering what the problem was each time I fell, she had already gone to her rest.

Now I was recovering after an operation in Beaumont with prospects of surviving into old age. Mary had not been so lucky. She would never grow old. She was one of the multitude that are taken out by cancer in circumstances so sudden that it can feel like a violation of the cosmos. I have no idea what pain her beloved Paddy was going through in those days when she got the dreaded prognosis, and what anguish he endured when, because of Covid, they were forced to speak to each other on screens.

For the rest of us, we forgot Covid the moment it was over. But for those who watched their loved ones endure the cruelty of isolation in their last days because of it, the Covid years will never be forgotten.

How did I miss it? Why could I not have remembered those things in the months before she passed, and have written to her? Almost everything can be said while someone is alive. When they are gone, there is nothing to say. Every wrong can be put right before the end. Every wound or hurt can be healed when people are in the full of their health. Every sin can be forgiven.

How did I not see it?

How do we always miss it?

I emerged from Beaumont after my operation on Good Friday of 2021. It was the second of April and it occurred to me that the following week would bring the first anniversary of her death.

I marvelled at how fast the years fly.

'My dear friend.'

That's all.

And the letter flies away from me and into the waste basket.

JULY 2021

To a Mentor of the Literary World

The first time I saw Bernard Loughlin's face I was afraid of him. He had big eyebrows, and though the expression was comical, it nonetheless contained a kind of seventeenth-century curiosity. He scrutinised people like Doctor Johnson might. He was the first and most extraordinary director of the Tyrone Guthrie Centre at Annaghmakerrig. He was appointed as it opened and he saw it grow and flourish, first as a writers' centre forging extraordinary links between north and south in the time of the Troubles, and later expanding it with studios for visual artists, larger parkland and exotic gardens. He served it fastidiously and cherished the manner in which its deep dimensions of collaboration and cross-cultural bonds were not only anticipating the Ireland that was to emerge a quarter of a century later, but in fact were an enormous cultural force underlying the societal change that Ireland desperately needed at the time.

But he revelled in the mythic memory of Sir Tyrone so much, that I imagined him almost as the heir to Guthrie's grandeur.

He lived in the house like he was at home. In fact that's exactly what it was. A home for his beloved wife and two children until he retired to the high Pyrenees to write a memoir of the light and the dark that constituted his life at Annaghmakerrig.

And he certainly loved the villages of the high Pyrenees too, where he found refuge in yet another garden.

And he also loved Donegal, where he had once worked on a fishing boat. Maybe that's why his face kept surfacing all through July. Almost 40 years after my first meeting him at Annaghmakerrig in late July of 1984. And knowing how worthy he was of praise, I realised, as I walked the beaches, that he had been far more than a mentor and friend and inspiration.

I had loved him too.

It was your daughter's voice on the phone saying you were gone that shocked me; calling you Benny. That's what broke me. Your face rose up again. I see it sometimes now at night.

And her face so like her mother's, and your son's face like the image of you; he carries your courage and integrity reinvented in a young gaze.

You were far too elitist to bother with popular culture so I could never imagine you using stuff like Facebook, but there's something about Facebook that makes voyeurs of us all, so here's a secret: I used to track your daughter's Facebook posts sometimes to see news of you.

She didn't know how much I was curious about you and where you were. What was life like for you in Spain after you left Ireland? What were you planting in your garden?

And then those peaks in the Pyrenees she posted, in summertime with blue skies and in winter with blankets of snow covering the village, and you with a red nose and a woollen hat and a shovel in your hand to scrape a pathway in the snow, and your huge bushy eyebrows laughing back at her camera. It's not that long ago when she was a child and you contacted me to see if I would perform a blessing at her wedding.

It might have been an embarrassment to me. Even though it might have been a great opportunity; the first chance to break the ice and visit you all in Spain. But the idea of officiating at a wedding bothered me. I wasn't sure of my ground because I had recently retired from active ministry as a priest. I didn't know how I felt about all that. It was too frightening. I was too raw. I didn't feel up to it. So I found some excuse not to attend.

But it was all about me. And what I missed was how you might be feeling at the time or how it might have mattered to you. Or how it might have brought some kind of resolution to your own private traumas and nightmares. I failed you then. There was so much confusion in me at that moment in time about religion and the church that I feared I would fumble at the feast. I wanted to distance myself from a church that even in 1984 I sensed was falling apart from systemic corruption. I certainly didn't want to get sucked back in.

But saying no let you down.

Yes, perhaps I was afraid that officiating at a wedding in such a beautiful place and on such an auspicious occasion and with people I loved might draw me back into the church. It might have exposed my regret at having left. It might have even shone a light on how self-obsessed a writer's life can be, compared to a minister of religion who spends the day going from one prayer to the next, attending to the mystery of how we cope with being human.

The religious ministry is a beautiful pathway and one that I will always regret not following. But I couldn't admit those things at the time. Instead I just made excuses; I wouldn't be able to say the right things. I might let you down. And any ceremony I conducted would not have legal status in the eyes of the church.

Oh yes, I had all the excuses. But when I think of it I laugh; as if you cared about the legal niceties or the jurisdiction of the Roman church.

And so in the end, and for fear that I would fail you if I was conducting the service, I did actually fail you all by not turning up.

How ironic when it was that same beautiful strong and courageous woman who took up the phone to call me all those years later. Who would have guessed that my first trip out to visit you in the Pyrenees would be to offer a blessing at your funeral. Or that your daughter would be the one asking me this time if I would officiate; conduct some ritual of farewell at your burial. I was no longer confused. I was in a hotel in Dún Laoghaire and I said yes instantly.

All those years ago I got an invitation which was an enormous privilege. To preside over the wedding ceremony of two young people. And I declined because of my own anxieties. How did I feel about the church? How did I feel about weddings outside the church? How did I feel about conducting a wedding service like an outlaw?

I was confused about me. And it was all about me.

When in fact it ought to have been about you.

You as a family were inviting me to share something and I couldn't see how simple that was. Maybe that's the source of the estrangement that grew afterwards. Because friendship is about showing up. Someone shows up for me, and then sometime later I show up for them. Behind the sentimental flavours of any family gathering, behind the fun and charm and leisure that family parties engender, there is a bottom line of friendship and solidarity and it's expressed eloquently in just showing up.

I still remember the day myself and the beloved were married by a priest in Galway, and I stood at the sanctuary half an hour before the ceremony, worrying if anyone would come. And then a shadow fell across the door and you walked down the aisle with your beloved Mary and you both took up the front pew close to the musicians and you said, 'I suppose this row is for family, but sure we're family. Aren't we?'

You showed up and it meant so much to us that you honoured us in that way.

'You're early,' I said. 'You're the first.'

'We came a long way,' you said. 'And we didn't want to be late so we gave ourselves plenty of time.'

And it was after that, believe it or not, that you asked me to come to your daughter's wedding and do some kind of blessing, and I refused. I can't even remember what shallow excuse I used. But the bottom line is that I didn't show up when you had asked me to.

It took me years to understand the Irish funeral. To see that the embrace of a thousand hands was not about individuals. It was about the entire community taking the weight of grief from the shoulders of the wounded and, in one collective family or community hug, sharing the grief.

Really sharing it.

And so showing up at a funeral, just to be in the crowd at the door, just to be in the back of the church, and just to shake a hand for a brief moment and mutter the words 'I'm sorry for your troubles' was both enough and essential.

And not showing up was a serious neglect, not of the dead but of the family grieving. I didn't show up at the wedding but I was certain that I would not make that mistake again.

When I didn't show up at the wedding it made it more and

more difficult as the years went on to show up at any other time. That, I suppose, is the way karma works. It's not just the single deed that matters, it's the fact that every deed initiates a new direction, a new trend or tendency or pattern that is easier and easier to repeat. Once you decide not to show up, for one single reason, it becomes much easier to not show up the next time. And eventually it becomes impossible to break the pattern and show up when you most want to.

But in the aftermath of the quake that your sudden death opened in the heart of your family, your daughter took up the phone and called me. After all those years when you were in Spain and I was so out of touch. Even though I might sometimes hear of people who had been visiting you and how much fun you all had, I was outside the loop. Because you did so much for me when I was young and because you helped me in my journey as a writer so fundamentally, I should have been there for you. And I wasn't.

And yet when someone casually spoke your name in a conversation, I felt a sense of physical unease in my body as if I belonged to you in some way. As if the time when our paths crossed was a space of permanence that had been abandoned by me, and I couldn't get back to it. You were like an elder brother who got me started in my chosen path, and on I went, and never looked back or returned to thank you. Life passes and I drift away from my deepest self.

And life on the surface is a constant drift from self. It makes me even now feel ashamed. And a shame felt particularly sharp when I went out to Spain to see you stretched in a coffin. To see the one I called brother, at rest, with your brow no longer furrowed and your great eyebrows forever stilled by the treacherous digger that flung you from the top of that cliff ledge just outside your home and down to the roadway below.

It was difficult to resist the urge to touch you. To say, 'Bernard, wake to see your children on my shoulder broken with grief.'

Your closed eyelids.

Contrasted with my memory of them sparkling.

Your silent lips.

Contrasted with my memory of your wit.

The tragedy of your sudden death, made even harder for them to bear because it happened outside the door of the house. Slipping over the ledge with all that dramatic scenery around you, the deep valley and the mountain peaks, and the sight of your funeral hearse coming in the distance, below in the valley, curving its way around the twisting zig-zag road as it climbed up the mountains to where your beloved and your children stood at the door, at the broken wall still marked by police tape where the accident happened.

The three of them isolated in the sunny mountains. Welcoming you home for the last time.

And I, who would claim you as a friend, knew nothing of the home you nourished there over the years. I even went about the house gawking at photographs that were framed on the mantelpiece and on bookshelves. Images of you in your mountain garden, holding big onions in your fist. Images of you beneath that soft hat, and leaning on a spade, and of course the most precious image of all: you sitting in an armchair, with a newspaper, wearing what looked like a dressing gown and clutching what might have been Christmas presents.

I didn't want anyone to see me gazing at them because it might have been too nosy. But you were just an old man in the mountains with a good pension.

Who could wish for more?

Your life summed up in a few photos on the sideboard, as the mourners gathered for your wake. Your smile surprising me on your daughter's Facebook page.

It's wrong to say someone lived. It's better to say that

they loved. And you had been loving for years, without me knowing or caring. And then I wanted to walk back into it, wanted suddenly to be part of it, just at the moment when it was over.

And why not write like this? Why not allow the table to provide the vocabulary and grammar of civility? Why not reach for words that embrace old ways of thinking, like love and forgiveness? Why not use words minted in an age of faith?

I will pray for you.

I will keep you ever in my heart.

The table was my anchor again. It afforded me permission not just to speak but to begin speaking in a manner that is unfamiliar in this age of materialism.

Because words can expand us, but they can also restrict us. It depends on what words we use. Put it this way: if we use the language of faith, hope and love, and speak in terms of divine realms, we begin to inhabit those possibilities. If we fence ourselves into an empirical landscape, governed by reason and logic, we eventually cease to experience the depth of being, the dreamscape of possibility beyond what is reasonable. Vast realms of experience may be consigned to non-existence if the language used to describe such states remains unspoken. The secular world trips me up in every letter I write. I fall into sentiment, transient affection, and emotional bravado. All those substitutes which the material world provides to replace the grammar of transcendence.

I scribble sentimental sentences:

I love you—

I have always admired you—

I have never forgotten our wonderful times—

I am sending you love—

I am sending you hugs, and good wishes, and lots of LOL smiles—

All I really want to say is that I pray for you. I hope you pray for me; because as long as we live, we are and will be the best, the very best, of friends.

You had invited me out on regular occasions. Yet I was convinced that you might have had enough friends, high-minded and erudite, famous and important. You had enough friends to bring you all the Irish rashers you required, to invigorate you with arguments about poetry and books. I didn't even feel myself worthy of all that august company.

It's funny how self-obsession can masquerade as humility.

Sometimes I met your daughter in Dublin. I'd say, 'Yes, I must go out soon.'

And she'd say, 'Oh Benny would love to see you.'

But it never came to anything. Until one Friday evening in November of 2018. I was in the Marine Hotel in Dún Laoghaire when she phoned to say there had been an accident.

The light was not long gone from the sky. I looked out the window and saw the harbour as a faint watercolour of grey gathering around the pier. Boats on the water and cars on land all parked in the same lifeless fog as the darkness seeped into the window frame and left me at last looking at my own image in the glass.

I must have been staring out for ages after she put down the phone. I saw the red brake lights and white headlamps of cars in traffic snaking along the pier road. I tried to imagine what had happened in the mountains but I couldn't. I had no idea what the village looked like, with its narrow streets like shelves one above the other, and the red-roofed houses with their arses stuck into the hill.

After my one-man show that night in the Pavilion I went early to bed and in the morning took a flight to Barcelona, where I rented a car. I insisted on a vehicle with sat nav so I wouldn't get lost in the spaghetti laneways criss-crossing the outer rim of the city, and the rental company duly showed me a Toyota with a Garmin on the dashboard. But as I got into the evening traffic the screen of my sat nav went dead and I discovered the Garmin was not charging. It died and left me stranded in four lanes of traffic.

I sensed my way like a cat and drove into the mountains like a boy chasing after something he loved.

And how well you looked in your coffin. How well the morticians had wiped away the bruises and left an expression of serenity on your face.

How lonely your beloved appeared.

Forlorn.

And your children standing at the door as the hearse manoeuvred the narrow streets.

Your brother Michael and a few close family members and friends carrying the coffin up the pathway to the front door where your son greeted his dead father.

Coming home, someone said. Coming home.

The little mannerisms of death.

And how poignant the ordinary world becomes in death. The small things on your desk, downstairs where the coffin was set on chairs and opened for neighbours to view, appeared bitterly ironic in their casualness.

The notebooks. The laptop. The pencils and a pen. Things that anyone could walk over and touch. Press a button and waken the screen of the computer and no doubt discover what last sentence you wrote just a few hours earlier, that morning perhaps before you went out to work on the garden and to sit on the bench and survey all the mountains with a book in your hand.

All that busy living you took for granted. And now the desktop and the implacable coffin spoke to each other. Argued with each other. It seemed unjust that you could not open your eyelids, or see the light of the lamp above you, or walk to the desk and continue where you had left off in mid-sentence only that morning.

But even in death I could feel his presence draw near, as they manoeuvred the coffin in the door and into his study, and left it resting on two chairs. The chorus of grief reached its crescendo as the funeral director opened the lid, left it idle in the corner, and then the procession of his family and loved ones began to come

to terms with this terrible absence that manifested before them in the wooden box. I went outside until the private liturgy was over and then much later, after mugs of tea and sandwiches, I went back down to the room and sat with him alone for an hour.

His face was marble, but the absence of any soul had been well masked by the morticians. His eyebrows bushy as they always were. His expression as lively as if he might jump out of the coffin. My eye scanned the room. His desk in the corner. Neat and tidy. His computer. And on a shelf I saw one of my own books.

I didn't cry.

Bernard was not a man you could cry over easily for fear he would appear behind you and subvert your grief with acerbic wit; at least in life his passions were not to be meddled with. His tongue was sharp. And only a few close friends understood that the wit was the gatekeeper to the tenderest of hearts. I felt myself absorbed in his death as a kind of contrast to being alive. Being able to breathe and stand in the chill of the house or walk outdoors into the moonlight or feel the heat on my face the following day was exhilarating; and like at every other funeral,

I spoke the usual words of consolation and extended sympathy to everyone concerned, but my heart was not in it.

'I'm sorry for your trouble,' I said a hundred times, and perhaps it's the effort to express such mannerisms that retains civility in the human heart, but alone with Bernard's remains that night I was full of remorse for my own neglect. How hard would it have been to write an occasional letter and share how I felt?

And no fragrance of this life will ever again touch your mortal body. Whether it be the taste of guava or a ripe tomato, good wine or fresh bread. Those rich flavours will never again penetrate or soften you, never raise the glow of life and happiness that I often remember in your eyes when late at night and after good food, we would open another bottle of wine at Annaghmakerrig and talk about Derek Mahon.

Oh how you loved Derek Mahon and that elegant poem 'A Disused Shed in Co. Wexford'.

You could recite it at three in the morning.

The guava fruit and warm bread are useless to you now, I know. But it always surprises me that not even poetry can protect us from death. Everything grows stale in the house of the dead, and sitting with you was like sitting in a locked room, from whence you could never again escape.

No music, be it banjo, cello or electric guitar, would ever again break the silence of death in your ears.

Your eyes would never again open to sights as beautiful as the high Pyrenees around you, or the far-flung ocean waves on the coast of Donegal near Carrickfinn where I once walked with you in 1989 at midnight, after the pub closed, and you recited verses by Pablo Neruda, from a book that I still have on the shelf.

Back then I had fled to Donegal in poverty and lived in a small chalet all through the winter, going once a week to Dungloe on the Lough Swilly bus to buy groceries and naggins of whiskey. I had holes in my shoes and was ashamed to be penniless, purchasing tins of beans in a local shop, because it was all I could afford to spice up my boiled potatoes. And you, being the director of the most important arts centre on the island, brought an enormous lift to my spirits when you drove to the door of the chalet I was renting, in your lovely blue-grey station wagon. And you brought such an army of comforters with you, a gang of creativity from the grounds of Annaghmakerrig. You brought Dermot Seymour and Leland Bardwell and Mary Loughlin.

Those were years of soft hats and tweed coats which endowed you with the air and grace of a gentleman. Your masculinity was like a big girl's blouse, as Mary Farl Powers used to say when she was drinking neat gin at the cocktail hour, in the bay window in Annaghmakerrig, with a wide-brimmed straw hat to shade her from the slanting sun.

'Big girl's blouse' wasn't a phrase that came easily to the lips of that high-minded Irish-American artist who could remember her childhood being infiltrated by great writers like Spalding Grey and other custodians of linguistic orthodoxy, and more than once she chastised me for my misuse of language, and my faulty grammar.

When I declared that you were 'a serious good gardener' she said she took no pleasure in pointing out that you were, in fact, 'a seriously good gardener'.

Anyway, you were amazing with a spade. And wherever she got the phrase from I don't know, and perhaps it was those dollops of Gordon's gin on which she floated into the dining room, but she did allege that you were indeed only a big girl's blouse.

Maybe a working-class boy from Andersonstown needed to wrestle with more than she imagined. A boy from Andytown in Belfast was not a predictable inheritor of Sir Tyrone

Guthrie's dinner table. Mary Farl Powers was at home in the sophisticated atmosphere that artists and writers could manage to engender around dinner tables, long before art became the weapon of activists and the institutions of high art were still fully dressed in their formal colonial clothes.

You certainly used full stops in your speech with great effect, both satirising the ruling classes and giving yourself time to compose the next damning phrase in an argument.

But behind the bravado, I think you were just a simple boy who wanted to run naked into the lake and splash about with a sort of wild fun. You had a relish for life that was infectious. A relish for onions, radishes and savoury cabbages. And so all your tweed seemed to both mock the mannered elites and enfold you like a baby in a blanket.

You taught me that there was a professional path for the writer. It didn't need to be a fog to wander in and it didn't end on a bar stool. Young writers in Ireland at that time still needed to learn those things.

You house-trained and refined me and so many other young writers of the time. And even when you came to Leitrim years later, and sat at the long wooden table we dined at in our little cottage, you were still pushing the envelope.

'Where do you actually work?' you inquired.

'Out in the back shed,' I said. 'It's my office.'

'It's a fucking coal shed,' you corrected.

'Well, I don't have a library,' I protested. 'This is a small cottage.'

But you were indignant. 'You can't be a fucking writer if you're writing in a fucking coal shed. You're undervaluing your art.'

In Annaghmakerrig you provided me, a young unlettered and unlearned peasant, with the wherewithal to focus on and value literature. And you taught me how to use the dishwasher.

That is precisely what you did for me; without having published anything or without having any confidence that I might become a writer, you showed me the standards that were required.

Yet when you moved to Spain I never saw you again. I ignored you ferociously and it was with shame that I saw on a shelf behind your desk a book I had written. It was with shame that I heard your daughter say she often brought you my latest work, or that sometimes when you were on the phone to her you'd mention something I had written in the newspaper.

I never darkened your door. Even though you were the one who had opened the door for me.

I suppose I thought there was always time. There would always be time in the future. And I would go out to the mountains on a visit – someday.

But the time ran out; there was no time left. I saw your son standing beside the opened coffin. We were just gazing at the marble countenance that remained. The stony serenity trimmed with coffin lace.

How could I have forgotten that life ends like this, and that there is never enough time to put friendship on the long finger. To know your eyes would never open again to sights as beautiful as the enormous tomatoes in your garden or the far-flung ocean waves on the coast of Donegal from where I am writing this now, or on the beach where we once walked, you, me, Cathy, Leland, Mary, Dermot, all together in a line against the dark wind; embracing each other and the night.

To remember you as you were then, hardly more than 35 years old, with wife and family, and to know that you can never hug those loved ones again. They can never put their arms around you. They can never get the taste of garlic in the air from your breath as you shower kisses on their cheeks. All the kisses gone. All touch and joyous breath. No more.

Forgive me for the long neglect.

I throw most pages in the waste basket. But sometimes I say no. I make an exception. Not that one, I declare, and I pick it out again and store it in the secret compartment of the Pembroke table. They don't bother me in there. And yet I have not destroyed them. Their content balances delicately between acceptable emotions and the embarrassment of committing myself to a feeling. That's what I'm bad at: saying how I feel.

But at least it was a beautiful funeral. In story and song we remembered you well. And in grief we opened our hearts to you one last time, and held you close, and hugged you with a hug that would last us for the rest of our days.

You wouldn't be seen dead in a church. You poked fun at the Christian tradition with all the mischievous wit of a character in a French novel, so I wasn't surprised that your funeral was to some extent a humanist affair. As the officiating person, I was careful to use no flowery religious words as I spoke at different moments in the process of conducting the assembly of friends in their remembrances, although it was ironic that the venue should be an old church. In some comedy of chance you lay exposed beneath a ghostly vault of garish saints and dusty flowers and flaking walls.

Yes, it was ironic, but perfectly appropriate to the true complexity of your heart.

Bernard hoped. And he knew that hope requires no naming. His faith needed no signposts. His flaws were obvious, and his love was existential. The hagiographer would call him a saint, living a life of contemplation in his garden. Because no matter how gregarious he was, and no matter how long he sat up with a bottle of whiskey, eloquently rejoicing in poetry or contentiously arguing about politics, he was always slipping away.

After dinner, or in the afternoons, when the crowd was gathered and the party in full flight, he always slipped away.

He would go to his man cave, or his garden, and entangle himself in clay and roots and weeds and fruit. In the unnamable sensate digging, as he dug into the mystery of being.

Sometimes he was present; forceful and argumentative and witty and occasionally wise. But then he slipped away again.

'I'm fading,' he might say, and go off to lie on his bed, or maybe to his office and hide behind the screen of his computer; but he always left first. And when he was absent people talked about him. In death too, he just slipped away again.

That's how I will remember him. He just left the room and might be gone for a short while.

We remain only for a short while. And then we too will be gone.

And then to join him.

AUGUST 2021

The gatherings of starlings on the electric wires along the road to Dungloe reminded me of an uncle who didn't like starlings. He'd be sitting at his kitchen table, as tranquil as an enlightened tai chi master, but then he'd gaze out the window, notice a starling on the bird feeder and suddenly he'd lep up, shouting, 'Bloody flying rats.'

He lived alone, and I was young and arrogant enough to not understand that little things become important to a person who is confined in a small space for long periods. And to a person who does not reach out and talk to other humans.

Now I'm almost as old as he was when he died. I was severely confined by the lockdowns but it was only when I was in hospital that I realised how little I communicate with old friends. Now I'm more aware of how small things can become obsessions to a solitary man.

For example, the song of the first cuckoo in April just after I was released from hospital was like milk in my ear. The bird was fresh to the singing. But after a while others arrived, bellowing across the lake, day and night, until eventually they all went hoarse, and sounded like dogs barking in the distance.

I had strong urges to shoot them.

And not every bird sings like a blackbird.

A few years ago a strange bird with an unusual little twitter started before dawn outside my window; just one single tweet repeated for hours, like a tiny persistent creak in a mattress. It kept me awake, and after a few days I began to understand what white Anglo-Saxon males mean about keeping a gun under the pillow.

I wanted to post my rage on Facebook, but someone stopped me.

'You're unwell,' they said. 'You must never tell people you want to shoot small birds. You're just getting things out of proportion.'

One morning I was distracted from my obsession

with the little balls of twittering feather outside the window, by a video call from a friend in London.

'Have you heard the birds these mornings?' she wondered. 'Are they not just wonderful!'

'Oh yes,' I lied, 'they're utterly amazing.'

She was so enthusiastic that the next time I was shopping in Aldi I bought bird seed.

Then I went into the attic and found a telescope attached to a tripod which I once bought for a video camera but could never manage to connect.

So I scattered the seed, and positioned the telescope on the patio.

But the birds insisted on aggravating me further; because they never touched the seed unless I took my eye away from the lens. When I stood up to go into the house they descended on the seed and fed like ravenous turkeys. But as soon as I got back to the lens they all flew away again.

My friend from London called again, in tears.

'I've split up with Robin,' she declared.

I thought she was winding me up, until I remembered her boyfriend's name actually was Robin.

'That's terrible,' I said.

She described his lack of attention, his long absences, and not least a recent infatuation with another woman.

'Have you thrown him out yet, or did he just go?'

'He just didn't come back,' she replied, 'from Bristol. And then he sent me an email.'

'How are you?' I wondered.

'Dreams are terrible,' she confessed. 'I was in a coffin, bound hand and foot. In another dream I was a young girl bricked into a wall. That sort of thing.'

'Maybe you have Covid-19,' I suggested.

'I don't think the virus induces nightmares,' she said.

'I wouldn't bet on it,' I replied. 'If the walls of nursing homes had ears, and could speak, I suspect they would record a grim account of human dreaming.'

I tried to get the conversation around to my telescope and the birds in the garden, but I felt like a self-obsessed child compared with what she was suffering so I decided not to say anything.

And that's the problem. I never say anything about my feelings on the phone. I never send letters. And it was only in hospital, isolated and frightened by an impending operation, that I realised how over the years I had isolated myself in a room with a keyboard, talking to people in general on a podcast, or on the radio, or in newspaper columns, but never quite managing to cherish the real friends around me.

This doesn't apply to the beloved, with whom I have a relationship that is on another level entirely. It's almost ontological the love that envelops us, but a marriage needs other spaces and other levels, where the couple can go separately to share who they are in a wider circle.

The starlings who had been aggravating me in Leitrim during the lockdown by lodging on the wires around the house stopped singing when rain came in from the west. In their stead two hooded crows arrived, ate all the seed and settled in the trees. I was incensed. But I scattered more seed, hoping the finches and tits might return.

Hours later I was sitting at my desk when two long black wings glided across the garden, and the hooded crow dropped an enormous dump of skittery white poo on my telescope.

'Shite! shite! shite!,' I roared, as I leaped up in rage and ran towards the door.

And now on the beach I hear only gulls. But I remembered my uncle, how gentle and saintly a human being he was; living alone, feeding birds, and patiently reading his way towards death with cancer.

And it struck me that he may have been more lonely than he ever admitted, or than I had ever realised. And perhaps I had been more lonely than I admitted, as I wrestled with birds like they were demons come to torment me.

To an Old School Friend

I've just about got through the summer and there's very little improvement in my condition. This leg is slow to heal. And the guts are not right. I'm in agony sometimes doing things that any human over four years of age would consider normal. I haven't told you the gory details before but let me spell it out, because it's gone on for six months now; I can't go to the toilet without taking a serious quantity of chemicals. I take painkillers every day and still my legs screech with pain. It's like being flailed with nettles from morning to night.

And yet there has been slow progress and it's astonishing how elated I get with the slightest improvement.

No wonder I'm turning back to religion. How could I not be grateful? For the time being I have escaped serious or permanent damage to my intestines or legs. They tell me I will recover. Maybe not totally, but there is a lot of healing yet to happen.

They promise me.

And so I'm patient.

Sitting by the ocean and writing letters. And staring at the dying sun in the evenings.

It's getting shorter now. The summer is over and the light fades faster each evening.

And thanks for letting me know about Declan's death. You know every time your name comes up on my phone nowadays I wonder who else has kicked the bucket. Not that I knew Declan very well; that eccentric genius who once worked in a coalmine, and was in our philosophy class in Maynooth and then ended up as a school caretaker. There's no telling why some people keep to themselves all their lives. But Declan was one of those. Always smiling back then, and yet forever an enigma. There was no telling what he was thinking. *The Irish Times* in the pocket of his jacket. As if it was a passport.

I got the feeling even when we were all in our early twenties that he was an elderly man on the inside. His race was over from the beginning. He was retired since he was 21. And he was spending it in solitude. I saw the last of him back then but I know you kept in touch. Maybe that's the difference between us; you keep in touch with people. I don't.

But as you said on the phone, you never really got to the inside of him either. I suppose he was just one of those guys. They smile and are gentle and nobody will know what it looks like from their side.

And then a week later I got this message that another one, Fitzpatrick, had passed. I thought, Do you ever ring me when someone hasn't died?

I remember Fitzy in grey suits and full white collars which made him look more like an Ulster shopkeeper; something that my mother loved. She said he reminded her of her own father who had Belfast roots and worked across Ulster as a pig dealer for McCarren's in Cavan.

That was the time you drove to Glangevlin to visit me. I was living in the mountains at the time and teaching in Loughan House. The wild mountains of west Cavan. You came up in the company of Eileen, my American girlfriend in the Maynooth days. The dearest woman, she was.

And one night we were at a party in a country house up the mountain. A man in his late sixties had returned from America for a rare holiday to his homeland.

You sang 'Fareweel tae Tarwathie', which they found

bewildering, and then you went into 'An Mhaighdean Mhara', which we all knew back then from the Clannad album. And when you did 'Only Our Rivers Run Free' the entire kitchen was in your arms, loving you for voicing a kind of wound we felt on the mountain because we did our shopping in Enniskillen, and we always belonged to Ulster, and what they called the North.

But what I remember most is when the old man home from America started to sing. The smoke-filled kitchen was silent with the aroma of whiskey and tobacco and the attention was intense, as if at some religious ritual. His words like the drone of an organ, like a prayer. And at the end his head didn't exactly bow; it was more like it fell onto his breast in utter devastation and sorrow.

I never forgot it. There are various renditions of the song on Spotify but they're all rattled out like dance tunes. Showbands in the '70s were fond of recording it, when mass emigration was still an issue in Ireland and people quickstepped and waltzed around ballrooms in London, like the Galtymore or the National, with fevered glee, determined not to look back with regret.

But the man singing that night delivered the song slowly and in a sean-nós style. His singing was understated but offered a promise that defied the narrative of his own life. The song promised that when all the roaming was done, when the wars and adventures of life were over, the singer might return to his beloved. Be assured, the song seemed to say, that just as the fields grow white with daisies in springtime, so too we will meet again.

'Killarney and You' is a song of exile. A man longing to be home on the hills of his native land. A man so far away that he can remember not just the clover and the sweet fragrances of the mountain but the young woman he loved back then. It's a story with a long and deep history in the broken hearts of many emigrants. The story of the woman and the long-ago time for which the singer's poor heart is pining.

He was a dark-haired man in his sixties, who had a modest office job in a train station in Chicago, and he had saved to make the trip back to Ireland before his retirement. The chances of him ever being back again, as he got older and was reduced to his pension, were very slim. The words cut against the grain of reality or reasonable expectation.

It's not the only song about meeting again, when in fact the circumstances of the narrative imply that there will be no more meetings. Nobody worries about singing 'The Parting Glass' at a funeral or the inherent contradictions in the song; addressing the deceased and expressing the hope that we all will have one more drink, when in reality the person in the grave will never taste sweet whiskey again. Or nobody is bothered about the promise to meet by the river, as a congregation leans shoulder to shoulder on each other like a rugby scrum around the coffin of their loved one.

Some songs are sung at such moments when the words cut intentionally against the grain of death. Songs sung not despite but because it's clear that there will be no further meetings. And they all promise a future gathering. It's something that makes us human. Even when a man has travelled across the ocean to visit the grave of his mother who had been buried in Glan cemetery one month before he sang that lovely song in the kitchen.

As you often say, we have good memories.

This all began as a text. It quickly turned into emails and then letters. My school friend had that ability to hit me unexpectedly. Maybe that's because he uses texts, especially when he wants to send me death notices. He's like the town cryer, or a bell ringer announcing tragedies. And for some reason I have always been thinking of lakes when his name lights up on my phone.

Or else I have been at a lake. Or going to a lake. And he has always asked, 'Where are you now? Are you at the lake?'

'Just because I referred in one book title to staring at lakes, it doesn't mean that I spend my life on the shoreline,' I said to him in one reply.

But then I thought maybe he's right. Because there was a phase of my life which began with lakes, with staring at lakes as if I was saying farewell to middle age.

And now it's a new phase; I'm standing at the ocean, and looking out at the azure blue thinking about old age as a kind of waiting time on the shoreline. Staring at water and wanting to be embraced by the depth that emanates from below the surface.

And in the old days it felt as if I was living on the inside; the lake was inside me.

But not with the sea. The sea is on the outside. There's no mistaking that. It's as if the entire dream world that was inside me when I was young, like a lake, is now definitely on the outside.

It's here before me, waiting for me to come home. The metaphysical world has a thereness about it, the older we get.

The lake was a metaphor for something inside me and the ocean is a metaphor for something beyond me that calls to me all the time. I'll put it this way. Staring at a lake, I was bidding farewell to a younger me. But standing by the ocean's side, I'm wondering how to say hello to a future I cannot fathom.

In all the lakes between Drumshanbo and Letterkenny and in all the holy wells along the road from here to there, I found myself, forming and transforming. I found what was inside me.

But in the ocean I find the ultimate Beloved, the mysterious other who shadows me from the womb; and especially here before me in the wounded ocean. It's in the sky and in the clouds and it runs through my body like grace.

On Sunday I went to a headland. Changed into the swimsuit. Walked down the dunes. I couldn't resist the waves any longer.

This was as sensual as my first kiss, or the moment I saw embodied in human form the one I call the love of my life. But here at the ocean, if you are of the right age and have lived through enough anxiety, there comes a moment where each wave is the finger of that ultimate Beloved who is everywhere and in all things.

It's a very strange paradox that we hope in the future, especially when we have arrived at a stage in life when there is no future for us. And all our old friends are dropping like flies.

People's faith, long ago, in an afterlife, as it was called – a home in some heavenly realm – is often scoffed at nowadays as a simplistic notion, inculcated by manipulative religious institutions to keep people from the reality of their unfortunate lives; hope in a fairyland beyond the grave dampening down any enthusiasm for social justice or change in the social structures of society.

Dreams of heaven being a kind of opium to maintain the snoozing masses and allow the ruling classes to keep their status. But the people I remember 50 years ago didn't seem at all to be naive.

They knew what life looked like and they understood that it ended. A union man in Sydney or Camden Town was under no illusions about the predicament of the working classes.

It's just that they found enrichment in the metaphors and poetic language of faith, which then allowed them to live in the present moment with a rudder, an ethical meaning, and a sense of hope.

To say I live now in the present is to defy all obstacles. To say I live already now in heaven, in blissful communion with angels, is an act of defiance. That is the rudder. The counterpoint of hope in a time of darkness.

And it's a poem.

How can people not free themselves from the literal cage of empirical meaning?

The scriptures of world religions are not books of science. They are books of signs. They are the rudder of love, and love is another kind of knowing.

Hope in heaven in order to live well now.

I know hope is not rational. That's the subversive power of it, and the consequences of hope are not in the future but in the present moment.

The rational path ends with Beckett and the existentialists, recognising that life is indeed a ridiculous predicament between birth and death, an absurdity of meaningless suffering. The man from America who sang in the summer night in Glangevlin knew he would never be home again. Knew his old mother was buried in the little churchyard near the chapel without him being present. Knew that he would as likely be buried in the far-flung soil of America. You might ask, how or why was he able to do it? How did the sorrow of it not swallow him up, or what made him plough on regardless? I don't know, is the honest answer. Perhaps he didn't examine his own predicament too much. Or perhaps in the end we do all get swallowed by the sorrow of life. When we are old and hidden away in nursing homes. But at least I can testify that in that moment he did sing. And yet he sang with understated emotion. With a calm baritone voice that measured out the phrases to embody as much hope and faith as he could.

If all over the world and in all history people sing their joy in the face of oppression, how could anyone approach death with rational science and accept it? How could anyone fail to sing defiantly of love as the thing in the present moment that triumphs?

And that song is one of two things.

Either it is the meaning of the universe, built into the very fabric of creation, or it is the meaning that we as humans give to the universe; to our life and love in defiance of all mortality.

When I say my mother is with me, and is just beyond my fingertips, I'm not offering a statement of scientific speculation. I'm sharing the condition by which I live now.

It's called joy.

Like Rumi, the singer in the night was opening a space of hope in something that defies rational thought. A hope that we all sense when it gets dark enough.

Fuck it, but it's a pity you didn't go to Maynooth as well. You might have become addicted to this metaphysical babble like I did. And then I wouldn't have to write all this to you.

It was Maynooth that did the damage. What you learn when you're young never leaves you.

It was late when we finished singing that night in the mountain; me and you and the man from Chicago. Very late. Perhaps close to dawn when the party got as far as the quiet kitchen singing. I remember a young woman who had fallen asleep in a rocking chair, a scarf over her eyes. But the sounds of the old man singing woke her up.

I thought of Rumi.

'Don't go back to sleep,' he said. 'People are going back and forth across the threshold where the two worlds meet.'

The door is open. Don't go back to sleep. I heard an old man calling in the dark of night.

On the beach a couple was playing ball. This is good, I thought. We're nothing if we don't communicate. And then I looked the other way.

A woman walking alone. Gathering flotsam.

And other little clusters of visitors, Scotti, tourists, dotted about with their blankets, rugs and beachwear.

Then suddenly to my left, coming from the waves, three women in beachwear. They heighten my sense of being old and male. But nevertheless, on I went into the waves. First walked. Then knelt my arse into the salty swell. Greeted each wave until I found my torso was numb. Rejoicing.

This surprised me because it highlighted the illness. But it also opened in me a new attitude to each wave; one by one the waves came, and each time my greeting it was a prayer. The rhythm drew me out of myself. It invaded me too, sending messages through my body. Something akin to meditation. The water cleared out all other attentions as it took possession of me and demanded singular attention to the rhythm of the waves.

To a Lover

I'm going to do it again because I can't get you out of my mind. And I'm confessing to you before I begin that this letter is just sentimental ramblings of someone who is not long out of hospital and gets caught every so often by the past. It's a net and it pulls us in. It gathers us up.

There's so much I wanted to remind you of. The times we went to Clare. The times you wanted to go around all the holy crosses on the west coast. The time of the wild roses in Ennis, and the mad nights in east Berlin.

We definitely got around the world.

But where are you now? That's what I wonder. In solitude old friends rise up. And old lovers. Am I allowed say that?

You were the one.

Do you remember the morning we met for coffee in the Brandon Hotel after we had talked about having a reunion and later exchanged emails?

We should get together sometime if you are in town, your email said. So we did. And I was late, and that was the start of it. We were arguing like the decades had not happened. And I was struck, sitting opposite you, thinking that this coffee morning might be a mistake. We were not suited long ago and we would never be suited in any other lifetime for each other.

Yet we were there, sharing memories. And when the cold coffee was finished and I got up to go we came close, and even though it was the foyer, we held hands and then I kissed you on the cheek and that moment expanded so that we kissed suddenly and ever so lightly on the lips.

It was not what I expected. And the moment it was over, I needed to flee from the building. I went to the car park and turned on the engine and drove for a few hours before stopping, and before I could get your scent off my lips.

It astonished me. After years your scent was exactly the same as I remembered it and desired it. An old body remembering with the fire of youth. It was like walking back into another universe. It was like waking up after 40 years.

And I am so sorry that I carried your letters around all my life and I never even read some of them closely until recently. Those little yellow mustard-coloured pieces of paper.

I was afraid to say I loved you when we were young. Afraid to write it.

But let me spell it out now.

I love you.

Back in the house I searched in the bookshelves until I found your picture. Or the picture of the two of us, I should say, at the canal in Berlin, and you are wearing black jeans and a black jumper and your hair is wild.

I'm sitting on the edge, my feet dangling over and looking backwards to the camera. You are standing with hands in your pockets.

It's as if both of us are diffident, uncertain, and yet before the scrutiny of the camera we seem to be saying yes, this is us; this is how we begin, even though we don't know how it will end.

I held your photograph in my hand, remembering that first day in 1984.

I opened a drawer on the writing bureau and took out the other letters. I counted 12, written over a period of one year.

Letters that I did not read often enough at the time; though they were none the less precious to me, and they consoled me in a barren world.

You wrote with the flamboyance of a medieval romantic, often embellished with squiggles and curves and underlinings.

I cherished your encouragement, even though I never replied to a single letter, sensing that you did not require any communication from me apart from phone calls.

My memory was a place I could go to and inhabit. And that was beautiful. And sometimes I forgot about you for years, and took you for granted, but it was amazing how one of your letters always managed to fall from somewhere, or from between the pages of the very book I was reading at critical moments.

Here beside the ocean your appearance was unexpected. Your return to me was a surprise. As if you were gradually appearing. Your presence not conjured by anything I did or thought.

I began thinking about you more often. I began struggling with the possibility of writing to you. Of all my attempts at reconnecting with old friends and enemies, surely you were the most critical and urgent. You were the one I should be writing to.

I must write to you soon or not at all. I must tell you that I have rediscovered you, as you were then on the canal bank in Berlin.

It was Dympna who took the photograph. She was gracious like a nun and as light in her frame as a bird, and I saw how heavy you took her loss at the funeral, but yet the photograph remains. She did us a service that day in Berlin when she took the shot. She added to the narrative of love.

Often as summer turned to autumn, I found myself satisfied writing to the dead. People who had passed away were wrapped in the past and floated up in the dark before me. But you were not dead. You were in my life. Taken for granted. And so I never wrote.

I went on the back road behind the sand dunes of Machaire Uí Rabhartaigh beach, because it was so windy that I thought my hat wouldn't stay on if I walked by the shore.

And after an hour walking I climbed one of the sand dunes to the top.

The walking shook out all the memories and obsessions of the previous hours. The journey was one of forgetting.

By the time I was sitting on top of the sand dune there was no naming my condition; call it joy or heaven if you like. It's like experiencing a magnificent full moon or hearing a bird sing or noticing the complexity on the wings of a moth.

The previous days had been hot and dry. Now it was windy, soft and misty. I sat in a blustery heaven and I wondered suddenly, where is my beloved?

It's never a good sign to see a man alone in a car for too long; it's a sign of anxiety. A sign that he is about to do something silly. And there I sat after descending the dune, for too long, as I often do, until someone knocked on the window and asked if I was okay.

Yes, thank you, I'm fine.

I was just thinking of a woman. Just on the verge perhaps of writing to her; the one I never wrote to.

I turned the ignition, started the car and drove home to try another letter.

SEPTEMBER 2021

To an Old School Friend

I was sitting at the window on the morning of the equinox, 22 September, when a bird startled me. The sun shone through the window and I could imagine it shining into all the megalithic tombs at Loughcrew in County Meath, as it has done for thousands of years, on that same day. The equinox always inclines me to believe that the cosmos is a constantly recurring moment.

Not that the world feels permanent or stable right now. And with rising sea levels, fires in the Amazon, droughts in California and locust plagues in Africa, it's hard to avoid the possibility that there might be something much worse down the line. And that's even before mentioning Covid-19. In fact I'm so primed to expect the worst that even good weather in September felt ominous as I prepared for a phone call with my doctor.

Waiting to get through to a doctor can feel like being an astronaut in a far-flung orbit waiting to link up with Earth in order to discuss something urgent with the experts.

Doctors remind me of how little I know about my own body, and though my urgencies are usually trivial mechanical matters relating to body parts, I always grow more anxious if the line remains endlessly busy. And when I get through I'm so conscious of other patients waiting their turn on other lines that I rush what I have to say and forget the key issues. Unless I write them down beforehand.

So there I was at the desk with a notebook, a sore elbow, a tingling in the left leg and a numbness in various other quarters. I was wondering if I might be deficient in vitamins, or if the tablets I take for various conditions were causing side-effects, when into that world of agitated emotions came a little bird.

I'm susceptible to mystical experiences at any time of the year, but the equinox is particularly auspicious. It marks the beginning of the long slide into winter darkness. And it's no accident that Rosh Hashanah, the Jewish festival of new year, falls defiantly around that time, when the musical notes of the shofar call the world to be made new again.

The shofar is a musical instrument, a long horn used in rituals to call the faithful away from all mundane realms and into that which lies beyond and is transcendent. The music of the shofar calls us to attend to the pulse of Being itself, which according to most wisdom traditions is made manifest in our hearts as our most intimate self.

I guessed it might be a robin, and when I put my head out the door I was proved correct. Perhaps the good weather confused him, or maybe he sings to himself for the same reason I play the tin whistle in solitude: it gets me through dark winters. Or perhaps there was no reason for his spontaneous joy, pouring itself into the world and opening for me a layer of optimism that cannot be described in words.

In a poem as brief as it is exquisite, Patrick Kavanagh once addressed a blackbird with the following sentence:

O pagan poet, you
 And I are one
In this – we lose our god
At set of sun.

It was morning when the bird surprised me and drew me away from the mundane world of doctors and medical anxieties, but that tiny little creature, on the branch of an apple tree, startled me no less than Kavanagh's blackbird.

And I could understand why Kavanagh addressed him as a pagan poet, because I too realise with increasing clarity that the natural world is a sacrament beyond anything that the liturgies of religious traditions are capable of expressing.

In the birdsong I could imagine the true heart of the universe emptying itself, and uttering itself in the quiet morning air. And I was astonished that one solitary bird in the garden had the power to lure me away from all my worries.

There he was, his perfectly round eye engaging mine.

I bade him welcome. Because I know that if things get darker in the next few months, with extreme weather or flu epidemics, or further surges of coronavirus, or even in moments of personal depression, his presence outside my window will be for me an enormous comfort and reassurance.

To an Actor

Tom Hickey was one of the greatest actors of his generation. His performances in Tom Murphy's *The Gigli Concert* and MacIntyre's adaptation of Patrick Kavanagh's *The Great Hunger* and *The Gallant John-Joe* were acclaimed as outstanding. And he created the iconic role of Benjy in *The Riordans*, a soap opera of rural life that enthralled the country for over a decade. He was diagnosed with Parkinson's disease in 2013.

I saw an image of you in my old photos yesterday. It came up out of the blue on Facebook. I don't like the way Facebook does that normally; it tries to bamboozle me with emotions and sentiment, for some reason. Here are your memories, the screen says. And I say fuck you, I'm not going to let you choose what my memories are.

But then you appeared, your back stretched as in a bow, the old clothes of Patrick Maguire hanging from you like flags in the wind, your head reaching up to the clouds; it was you, yes, in your role of Maguire, from that play *The Great Hunger*, and I couldn't figure out why Facebook was sending me your image. It was five months since you died and I read again your obituary, but I still didn't understand why Facebook would chose to remind me of you at that particular time.

You were the kind of person who would have said, 'Run it by me before it goes to print.' You had a watchful eye on publicity. But of course it doesn't concern you now. And then I thought, I must write to you. Even though it's too late.

Five months since I dragged myself to the funeral in Kildare and stood in the church car park as the cortege arrived, followed by the president Michael D. Higgins and Sabina his wife, who both loved you greatly. All around the stone walls of the car park were famous actors and people I knew years ago, but I didn't speak to any of them. I was too down with my own worries and trying to recover from the operation in Beaumont.

And this morning, it was as if you were alive again, somewhere out of sight, and I could almost hear your laughter.

Like you, I carried Mother around with me for a long time. When that happens there's part of you wakes up some morning in your sixties and realises your life was wasted. It's partially true for everyone, I suppose. Mine too was squandered on useless emotions.

It's just that we all think our own little loss is the most tragic; that our own damage is unique. Our own little wars are the most significant. And we fight them over and over again, for far too long. That's what changes when we age; although it's a pity that nobody tells us that when we're young.

I blamed my mother for holding on to her grief for too long. She hugged her pain, the loss of losing a husband, and she died feeling wounded and hurt, because she felt her life was what other people did to her.

But in fact, she did it all to herself. As Margery Cross explained to me when I first got curious about Buddhism, we are all responsible for our own lives. My mother endured until her nineties before anyone came from behind the Milky Way to steal her life, although she had spent many of those years feeling that someone else had stolen so many lesser things from her – purses were but one example of the losses that wounded her.

The first purse she lost was pink; she'd placed it under the pillow in her dormitory on the first night of her sojourn in a boarding school near Mullingar.

In the morning it was not there.

She accused all and sundry. First her enemies. Then when they had rationalised to her that they were not even in the dormitory she began blaming her friends. By lunchtime she was eating alone in the ref, and by the time classes were finished for the day she had considered the possibility that it was one of the teachers who crept into the dorm the previous night because the purse was so pink and pretty and because there were three crowns inside, ancient coins that her father had placed in her mother's palm on their wedding day and that were, in Nellie's eyes, perhaps the most priceless artefacts in the western world apart from the crown jewels.

And if it was the teachers who coveted the treasure and ransacked the pillow that she lay sleeping on, then it was a double crime for it had led to her accusations, and then losing her friends, and in all, when she surveyed the first week in school, it had been a disaster. She wrote home to her father that she was unhappy and would not stay a week longer in the miserable kip, and her father, being as pliable as a thimble on her sewing finger, arrived in a pony and trap from Castlepollard, at the doors of the college the following Sunday afternoon. Thus ended her formal education but not by any means her problems with purses.

That's how I would fictionalise her if this was a story. Although the essence is true. And that she found the coins in her own suitcase when she got home is undisputed, though she told nobody. And I believe they are the same coins that sit in a little pink purse on my shelf as I write this.

There's the story of a life; the keeping of things. The robbing of things. The injustice of the world. And the final awakening to the fact that it's all been a kind of delusion and trick of the universe.

I'm telling you this so you know that I understand where you came from. I know your mother was hard and, as you said to me one time, you could write a book about her. But not now. All that you said is now silence and secret.

My mother was once fortunate enough at 80 to be offered sheltered accommodation in Omagh, with a modern kitchenette and compact lounge, a quiet bedroom and glorious bathroom, properly equipped for a person of her age. Sheltered apartments with nursing care just outside the door. And she was discovered one day mooching around the floor under the bed when I knocked and called her name.

'I'm in here,' she said.

I looked down the corridor at the open door and saw her

two feet sticking out as she stretched herself flat on the floor to grab something against the wall beneath the bed.

Eventually she emerged and got herself erect, though not without some difficulty and much cursing, clutching in her hand the wrapping of a chocolate bar.

I asked her what she was doing and she explained that her purse was missing.

My heart sank.

'My purse,' she stressed again, 'with everything in it.'

Everything.

'Those fucking bitches,' she said, meaning the staff of the centre who had access to the apartment day and night while she was asleep or awake, to monitor her and to make sure she was well and sitting in the chair and had not fallen down dead on the floor.

It was a beautiful facility for the elderly, and all the other residents on the corridor seemed content.

'Those fucking bitches,' she said again, and that was the end of it. Or rather the beginning. I knew it would not be long till she was on her way home.

She insisted I take her home. And, disregarding her integrity and rights to independence, I stayed away from the centre for a few weeks in the hope that she would reconcile herself to her fate. But one night my phone rang and it was her.

'I'm home,' she said, triumphantly. She was calling from Cavan. 'I got a taxi,' she said coldly, and put down the phone.

I'm telling you this because I presume you too had a mother who loved you and wounded you. That's the nature of life. We're not perfect, and we wound each other wantonly.

But like all artists you made something powerful and beautiful out of the wound.

I sit at the rocks overlooking the waves, watching two lovers in the distance, walking the strand and holding hands. I feel it's so important to always be in love. Always stay close to the beloved. That's the leap that frees us from Mother; the fact that we walk away into the air and find her. Her or him. It's just that for me it was her. I recognised in her instantly a manifestation of the Beloved.

The lover that all longing is longing for. Reminding me of the face I had before I was born. And with that face I saw her. And her presence afforded me a cloister and affirmed in me the cloister that already had been built in the heart.

And I grew to love the poetry of Rumi.

I remember the night yourself and Tom MacIntyre came to Derrylin, the loveliest of parishes on the shores of the Erne in south Fermanagh, where I was a curate. But it was a place of turmoil and war beneath the surface, the lovely fields steeped in the blood of murdered innocence, and you both came to get the flavour of that intimate struggle – neighbour against neighbour – and to meet people who had suffered on both sides, and hear stories of shootings and funerals and grieving widows and women who had husbands in Long Kesh. We visited people in the vicinity of the parish and then went across the river to meet more in Lisnaskea. And on the way back the UDR stopped us on the bridge near Trasna Island.

'Good evening, reverend,' the soldier said to me. 'Could you tell me who are your passengers?'

'Patrick Maguire,' you chirped up, in a flat Monaghan accent, just as you did in *The Great Hunger*.

'Where are you from, Mr Maguire?' the UDR man inquired, noting something odd about your delivery and the quiet chuckle.

'From anywhere and nowhere, guard,' says you.

He wasn't amused.

We were stuck for half an hour of unpleasant conversation,

and I chastised you when we were finally let off into the dark towards Derrylin.

'I have to live here,' I protested. 'You can't be taking this as a joke.'

The fact is, you took everything as a joke. And it amazed me how much MacIntyre learned on those nights, and how the stories wove their way into his play *Rise Up Lovely Sweeney*.

You looked lonesome in a wheelchair at his funeral.

As an actor you must really go beyond yourself. But it could take years of only half-completed fits and starts. Like the little boy running after swallows with wellingtons that are too big for him. Suddenly chasing after every ecstasy. Every perfect thing calls us to our own eventual obedience.

I remember seeing athletes on television at the Olympic Games. Making perfect circles on the ice and then up into the music and the wind; as sure as larks. And I have felt that is how I'd like to be. But in a different way. Perfect and full of grace.

A sort of rhythm which gives everything its place. Like herons drifting easily over reeds and ferns. And petals never noticed beneath the brambles in the ditch.

With everything in its proper place. I go beyond myself at last as I and they obey.

You were the best man at my wedding. When the service was over we went to the pub; Costellos' galvanised shed with a cement floor and a pot-bellied stove. Mary McP was holding her recently born baby girl, proud as punch. Bernard Loughlin bought you a drink, you were on white wines. We sipped gently. We had to drive to the reception, which was in Roscommon, in the house we were going to live in. A house party with Mary playing the music.

Bernard and you got into detail about the performance you had done of *The Great Hunger* in the stables at the back of Annaghmakerrig, replete with living cattle in the byres behind your acting space, mooing through the show to indicate either their hunger, displeasure at the glaring lights, or just because they loved theatre.

And then Pat arrived, the legendary priest who had officiated at the weddings of so many estranged Christians or lapsed Catholics. He had a Black Bush whiskey with Coke and Bernard took umbrage, saying that nobody in their right mind would contaminate such a great libation by flooding it with Coke.

I didn't expect all of you to go so soon. Mary had cancer. Bernard had a tragic fall. And you lived quietly with Parkinson's, withering slowly before our eyes.

The night was your world, Tom; I saw you as the ghost of a great clown come from Europe to haunt the little provincial world of Dublin. I even remember how shocked I was when I first saw the sculpture outside the national theatre in Bucharest which depicts in bronze a cart-load of clowns and thought to myself that here on a surreal cart-load of clowns is where Tom Hickey ought to be remembered.

It was such an honour to be in the same rehearsal room as you. The man that Paul Durcan celebrated in his poem about *The Gigli Concert*. Because you were the one who had collaborated with Murphy in the first production of that monumental drama.

You were the one who collaborated with MacIntyre to create *The Great Hunger*.

The actor who more than any other actor had been in the first production of first plays by new writers; because you believed in writers. You believed fundamentally in the writer as life-giver to theatre.

But you were a volcano of arguments inside. And you kept it hidden and it fuelled ferocious creativity.

Was there something jagged and incomplete about our friendship? Or was it really friendship? Maybe it was just a mother thing which drew me to you, or that ability of yours to turn the rage into artistic fire. Or was there something in you that I despised because it was in me too?

All those questions lie unresolved when two people drift away from each other, as we did. And how quick the small ornaments and old postcards turn yellow in storage boxes and how easily the times we had can be forgotten.

For example, I remember going to see you on stage in the West End. I was looking out a hotel window at the blue skies of London listening to the bells of St Paul's Cathedral up the street, calling me to prayer.

I lay on the bed, reciting poems by Wordsworth, and later I walked up into the cathedral and considered for a moment the prospect of becoming a Protestant.

But what trapped me and you, Tom, in a Catholic cocoon was the incense and the sanctuary lamp. We grew up with that lovely red light, as comforting as a candle in the window at Christmas.

We grew up in clouds of incense as alluring as the aroma of Mother's apple tarts, wafting from a warm oven long ago.

For me the sanctuary lamp was the concrete manifestation

of the invisible; a magical world intruding into the banality of a Cavan childhood.

The lamp hung like a pendulum, from the high dome, flickering in mid-air above the altar, and whenever the oak doors opened, a sudden wind would flurry down the aisle causing the sanctuary lamp to shudder; it was an act of nature that would have silenced Job.

And the white wafer that floated above the head of the bleary-eyed priest at the mass, in a cloud of his own aftershave, was not merely a sign or symbol, but the very bread of angels.

I could never understand the cold stones of Protestant space; the indifferent walls, the pale windows, the blank and anonymous cross on the bare table.

The broken Jesus, stretched between the nails, thorn-headed and bleeding, was a token of love, just as precious to me as my one-eyed teddy bear.

Wittgenstein said that religious behaviour was like kissing a photograph of the Beloved; but in my Catholic childhood it was not an image but the real presence that touched my lips and tongue, and cleaved to the roof of my mouth, as I swallowed God.

In St Paul's Cathedral there is a side chapel, where people sit and pray.

I went there and sat in the dark mahogany pews, daydreaming, and quite unexpectedly the emptiness of the space enveloped me in a comforting and graceful manner.

The stark room was as exquisitely chill as a Zen temple might be to a person who has lived too long in the garish dazzle of Tibetan iconography, and in that empty vault I began to appreciate the sophistication of Protestant faith.

This mildly ecstatic moment, even before I had imbibed a Starbucks coffee or a sticky bun, set me up for the day to enjoy London as if I belonged in London, or as if London was indeed Jerusalem.

And that evening I went to see you, the great actor Tom Hickey, performing in Beckett's *Endgame*; a play in which destitute humanity makes an eloquent declaration of revolt about the existence of God.

You were playing Nagg, a legless character imprisoned in a dustbin, whose head emerges at regular intervals to gnaw at a bone or offer a gesture of affection to his lady companion, who lives in the adjoining bin.

The text was beautiful, and I never saw the savage roar of Beckett's anger and despair quite so eloquently made flesh, as by the gifted Mark Rylance.

I stood at the stage door later, as rain lashed the roofs of taxis. Up the street, outside Bistro Italiano, two waiters in black shirts and trousers were on a smoking break. They argued furiously with each other about who was the boss.

When you emerged from the stage door you were distraught. I inquired what the matter was.

You explained that as you were coming down from the dressing room to go on stage, the lift broke. You were trapped inside. You could hear the voices of the other actors performing, and knew your cue was coming in a matter of minutes but you could not break free, until finally a carpenter extracted you from the lift, inserted you into Nagg's notorious dustbin and delivered you to the stage, just in time for your first line. The play continued seamlessly, without the audience being any the wiser.

We dined that evening on battered haddock in a restaurant up the street and joked about your ordeal. And then you headed for the underground and I walked back up Fleet Street.

The bells of the cathedral tolled for midnight, but all I could hear in them was the magnificent and austere chime of an indifferent universe.

I'm sorry I didn't visit you often enough when you were in the nursing home on Orwell Road. I went once, walking up the road with Google Maps open on the phone guiding me, and thinking it was appropriate that you should die on a road named after that magnificent writer.

The nursing home felt tight and small and you were in a space with a stranger, which upset you, and you stared out the window at a few trees and told me you were writing poetry. Your body was shaking and you hadn't the energy to stand up. And you were enraged by the weakness.

The reunion didn't last long. I sat in silence for most of it, watching you as you stared out at the trees. I wished you could have cried or that I could cry. I wished that one of us was soft enough to feel something in that moment.

I suppose it's the tragedy of leaving things until it's too late. When the bedside becomes the waiting place, and the grim reaper is as near as the trees outside the window, something in the heart goes numb and all the things you planned to say at various times are frozen over.

I saw you lying in bed, with your head on the pillow, in an astonishing clip that Alan Gilsenan recorded shortly before you died. Your final farewell was an artwork in itself. Alan loved you too, and his film of *Eh Joe* by Samuel Beckett with you and Siobhán McKenna haunts me now as I grow older.

I watched *Eh Joe* again after the funeral. The close-up of your left eye as a tear falls out. And then and only then did I cry.

Because as usual it was beautiful. Magnificent. What you did on the stage and on screen was beautiful, even though you struggled so hard alone to make it happen on the outside.

There is a Sufi story about a butterfly. Male or female, it is not yet born. It is in the cocoon, and a young boy sees it struggling to get out. So the boy gets his penknife and cuts a slight aperture in the cocoon to help the butterfly get out. This works well and the butterfly then emerges without any further difficulty. But the little creature just goes to the floor and remains there, unable to fly. The struggle in the cocoon was what would have strengthened its wings.

Your wings were strong and you struggled a lot, escaping again and again from the same cocoon. I felt that your last years were the fiercest battle with ill health, but my hope was that it too would turn out to be a cocoon. Your last and final entrapment and your final and complete liberation.

I was praying for you. Watching you get ready for the road home and praying that you would find your way to joy.

And that's what I would have loved to say to you, Tom, as you struggled towards death. But I wouldn't dare be so provocative, so presumptive. Death is built into the universe like movement is built into the ocean.

It's after the storm that I think of Tom Hickey. When there is debris on the beach. Unusual birds taking shelter in the rocks. Dead crabs upside down on the sand.

The beach is like an empty house after a party where no one has cleaned up. And then Hickey appears at the far end of the beach. Or to be accurate he doesn't appear; but I can hear him laughing.

OCTOBER 2021

At night I sleep so soundly that sometimes I feel I am sleeping inside the mountain, underneath the mountain, and when I wake I imagine the men in old-fashioned suits who still inhabit my beloved's dream. And since the days are shorter and the nights stretch endlessly, I feel them in the house again, on their chairs along the wall. Just sitting like fair witnesses to all that passes.

There is nothing more comforting than bedtime when I am ill; to sleep in the shadow of the mountain, resting my back against Errigal so that I sink deep into its rocks as I face the coming winter.

It's still dark when I wake but I go to the kitchen

and slice an apple, mix it with some muesli and yoghurt and eat it, slowly.

Morning prayers in the Tibetan fashion.

I pray for those who helped to grow the fruit, and for the bees that helped to pollinate it and I pray that no animal was harmed, and that no human was oppressed by taking this food to my table, and I pray that by eating the food I will be kept alive another day, and that my life will end and then be repeated and I will remain forever, returning, as long as living beings remain and as long as I can benefit other sentient beings on their way to enlightenment.

And I pray for all those friends and lovers who have departed, and that we will meet again, and that, as Hickey would often say in rehearsal, 'we might do better the next time'.

After prayers I go to the sea to feel her fury after the storm of the night and watch again for stray birds like broken clowns, wandering the wasted landscape.

At the lip of the sand dunes I sense her presence as she wonders what she wills, and I wonder what this morning will be like when I finally get over the last hill and see her again, because it is always slightly painful to put off sleep, to shake off the night, to let go of the morning news and the ordinariness of domestic chores and allow her to drag me in, or drag me out perhaps. For she is definitely here.

In this ocean the cosmos is renewed and this beach is the cocoon that enfolds me, and when the time comes I pray to be released into the clean blue enamel of the sky.

To an Old School Friend

I feel more cheerful after talking to you. Even when you phone, and I'm just, like, listening all the time – and believe me, I haven't met anyone who can go on for so long on the phone. I mean, you talk non-stop. You ask questions and then you answer them yourself. You seem sometimes like you're talking to the therapist and when I think I might jump in and act the role for you I'm cut off because you jump in instead and become your own therapist. It's like being a fly on the wall in your head.

And sometimes I think your head is almost worse than mine, as a chamber of horrors. Not that I suffer much anxiety nowadays. I got over that ten years ago. But being morose is a bit of a cul-de-sac too and I travel it all the time.

Writing letters to people I loved who are dead; I mean, what could bring you down into the swampland of melancholy more effectively. But you have something else which lifts me up. You have this kind of ability to endure.

I'm not making a virtue out of suffering but you endure stuff that is appalling. I'll not go into it. You know what I'm talking about. You've had some hard knocks, and you always seem to be able to let it go.

I remember saying it to you one time and you said that it was because you grew up in a large family. Well, that's your view.

I grew up with one sibling and my father had one sibling and his father had one sibling so there were only six births on the male line in our tribe for over a century. At least you can't blame us for over-population.

But today I definitely need to write to you. In fact, if you phoned this afternoon, I'd be delighted. Not that I'm going to do anything as personal as suggesting you might phone. That would take us to a moment far too intimate.

Here's the story. I was morose. And I went to the beach, and while I was in the car park two women waved at me. I was delighted. A signal from another human being. So I walked over the sand dunes to speak to them. No, I raced. They said they recognised me because one of them had made me a sandwich the previous day. She worked in one of those mobile coffee vans. I said it was a delicious sandwich. The best sandwich I had ever eaten.

I talk like that when I'm starved of company. I go into hyperbolic mode, for laughs.

Anyway, she remembered me from the coffee van and now she was waving, and I went running over to the pair of them as if I was desperate to talk to someone.

I said I was staying nearby in a house.

'Will you be here for long?' they wondered.

'Maybe a few more months,' I said.

And then they walked off. I was devastated. I thought I was at the beginning of a long chat. You know the way in the old days we would meet a stranger and begin a conversation that lasted for hours. Those times when you forgot the clock. I did it in country houses, in bars and on the side of the road. In fact, I don't think people stop on the side of the road to talk to each other anymore.

So that's what I thought was going to happen. Me and these two women in the sand dunes talking all day. That's how deluded I am.

They turned their backs and continued their walk and I went off into my own private world, my own private beach in a way. Because the beach is that sort of thing; it's so vast that others shrink in size as you get further away and eventually become no different than seagulls and other shore birds. Just sentient beings moving like insects in the distance or in another world. But the world I inhabit now on the beach has more company because of the ancestors who walk with me.

I didn't tell you about the ancestors. You're not going to like this. It's a notion I have that there were 12 men in black suits and white shirts sitting on chairs in the house. It's an image in my beloved's dream. She told it to me. I picked up the image and decided that the house was the one I'm in and the 12 men are ancestors who have been waiting for me to come. Waiting for someone to inhabit the house again. Waiting for someone to pray for them.

That's fucked up, you would say; I know. But you know what my imagination is like so I'm not afraid to tell you.

Yesterday I found an abandoned lobster pot and saw a woman gathering stones. She must have picked up a dozen stones altogether, scrutinising each one – flat ones, I thought – and placing them carefully in a yellow rucksack.

After a while the bag must have become heavy. But she was far enough away so that I could scrutinise her. As I came close, I kept my eyes to the ground and to the ocean. There is something about etiquette on the beach that doesn't encourage me to be intimate or casual.

People seem more self-contained on a beach. It's very hard to intrude on their cosmos. Men with dogs. Women with stones. Women with each other, chatting. Families with more dogs. All in their own worlds. All on their own singular beach.

People like me with anxious eyes scouring the horizon for companions are rare enough. Because if there are lone males, they always seem to have a purpose. They always have contraptions or costumes, for kayaking or surfing or gliding. There's never anyone doing nothing. Which, I would have imagined, was the very pinnacle of meaning on a beach: to do nothing, be nothing, know nothing.

Oh but no; men must be busy. Busy, busy, busy.

Maybe it's like they're on the beach but in their heads they're not on the beach. In their heads they're doing what they do. They have identity. I am a surfer. I know what I am.

Or maybe their surfboards are a decoy and that really deep down inside they are actually doing what I do: enfolding themselves in the company of the ancestors, in order not to be entirely alone.

But there's one thing I haven't told you yet. And that is what I like about you. You see, it's okay to say it to people who are dead. I can really open my heart out to them. I say

I love you, and so on. It doesn't much matter, cos they don't hear me.

But you're still here. You're as healthy as a trout, you fucker. I can't believe how well you're doing at 69. But I can't imagine myself saying something to you that was as honest as how I speak, letter after letter, to the dead.

That's what I need to do. I need to write you an honest letter of gratitude for all the ways your friendship has been a support.

And will I do that?

Probably not.

To a Lover

I remember when we went to your house. It was a wet evening and the ditches were damp and the foxgloves were drenched and heavy. Up the narrow lane, the two of us on a bicycle, me on the back, which was surprising, saying I found you attractive.

And slagging you about who lived there. That it looked derelict. So we turned the corner and there it was, the stone house; you and me in your father's mansion.

He purchased it, you said, and made it his base, and I saw that it was beside the church and yes, of course I remembered, your father lies in the graveyard there.

Great place to bury him. Out at the corner, close to an oak. I'm surprised the church allowed you, says I.

And later, do you remember, when the curry was simmering, we went to the back of it and you showed me the tree, and the stone. And I took a polaroid picture of you leaning on it, that summer evening, and later in the house you showed me the urn.

'I couldn't get rid of it,' you said.

I didn't understand for a moment, until you explained that he had died in England and was cremated and that it was the ashes that came home to the oak tree.

'Do you keep anything in it now?' I wondered, and you looked like a Cavan lake on a winter's day, because you still cherished the sanctity of that empty space, that bowl of Buddhist blue in which your father's ashes were, and from which they were gone. 'An empty pot is a potent sign,' I said.

We made love on the futon in that mezzanine. We stepped through it like the grammar of a delicate essay and swept ourselves around each curve in the text like true aficionados of style and good taste, and when it was over the world appeared like a full stop.

And when we were finished you said, 'By the way, we never told the priest that we buried the ashes there.'

'How did you get away with that?' I wondered.

'We told him it was just a memorial stone we were putting up.'

Going down for the curry was like a new chapter. A new paragraph. As if I had just landed. And you would never say how you felt.

I grieve for the youth I was, the health I had, the fire that was in me long ago. And as age increases, I turn melancholic.

It is only when I turn the grieving into longing, and when the longing turns to God, that I begin to understand that loss and grief are doors into the depth of being, and that wounds are indeed places where the light gets in.

With Rumi, my soul is longing for the Lord, more than the watchman for daybreak.

That's my secret.

I say the words now to the hairy horse.

I believe in you.

I am no Christian.

I am no Jew.

No Buddhist, nor follower of Islam.

I am not from east, or west.

Not of the land.

And not of the sea.

My place? Placeless.

My trace? Traceless.

And sunlight dancing on the ocean like a mirror.

Your default position was to stay close to the invisible and say nothing. Mine was to stay close to you, the anchor of my heart.

I was in theatre because each play seemed like a liturgy. But it took a few years for me to establish a career of plays and one-man shows and then the endless tours around the country, wandering in solitude here and there, and you being always the reason I started out.

Always the reason I finally rounded it up and took down the tent. Wondering why I was doing it.

Meeting you was like meeting who I should be. But my imitations were inadequate. If only I could be with you and still be able to hold hands with God, like a child holding the string of a balloon, I would have been happy.

I never told you that before but there you are. It's never too late to say something new.

Yes. That is how I felt when I travelled with one-man shows. I felt I was wandering the roads like an orphan.

The worst time of all was when I performed a show called *Swallow* and you were at home and we would talk on the phone before the show.

I might be in a dressing room in Thurles or Portlaoise, Tralee or Waterford, and the posters on the walls would remind me of you. There was always some singer who had been on stage the night before me, and I'd hear the lighting designers saying how wonderful she sang, and what a great crowd was there for her. And it was humbling like in the way that salt on a wound can be humbling to the flesh.

And that's when I would call you. Just to hear your voice. Before the show.

Swallow was a short drama about an old Monaghan farmer who was broken by various tragedies and him standing in an empty hall on his land feeling like an orphan, cut off from his Orange culture north of the border. Feeling like maybe he should go wandering the roads because nobody loved him and bad things happened to him. Yes I know, it was floating in the same territory as my own sad self.

The performance lasted 40 minutes and you never saw it because of your own tour. In fact I never told you much about the show. What mattered was always our summers in that house of your father, where the foxgloves went mad, and the scent of meadowsweet wafted through the kitchen window, and we were caught one day on the kitchen table. Not that there was much of a kitchen. The house was almost one single space after your father broke the walls down, and the table came from Galway I think where you bought it for five pounds at the time, and it stood on the cement floor and you were so proud of it that when I arrived that evening, all of a sudden and unexpectedly you asked was I staying the night. I said if I'm allowed, and you cooked pasta and when we were finished and the dishes had been put away and the wine was almost gone, it came on us, as it often did, unexpectedly; this desire, this sense of the horses being loosed and permissions granted for everything the imagination could muster in the pursuit of intimacy.

Those were not prosaic moments, and there was nothing could be done afterwards but sleep with the windows open until dawn. But on that one occasion I think it was the priest who arrived and we joked afterwards that you couldn't make it up.

Hickey used to say that when something real happened, something dramatic and real, down the country in some shop or library. 'Look at that,' he would say. 'You couldn't make it up and you couldn't act it.'

That's how we felt when the clergyman was gone. He had almost caught us *in flagrante delicto* right there on the table, but we zipped up and gathered up and offered him coffee and whiskey and when he was gone we thought, *Holy fuck, we need to be a bit more discreet.*

Anyway, I still remember those afternoons, when I searched for myself like a dog after its tail until you broke the circle of self-obsession and gave me an object that was truly worth desiring. You were the other, the far-away planet, the hidden heart in the cosmos. The Beloved.

Is this me? I wondered, as I became aware of my body reflected in the light of your presence. Is this how lovers awaken? Do they begin to see themselves in the mirror of another body and learn to pronounce the word 'beloved'?

Is this me? I ask still, as I hear the October winds around the house and in your absence, even now, taste that summer long ago. The rich purple orchids and the flag irises.

When we were in our twenties, and we could still toss ourselves over the sand dunes like children, and how we marvelled at the light glistening on the ocean or how we swam like dolphins in the shallow water, coming out with the sand coating our bodies and making it difficult to kiss.

The beach interested you. It always will. Because the waves are still there. They were there before we arrived. And when we came in the night, after the pub, they were there in the darkness. The waves were there millions of years ago. The waves have witnessed so much that has passed. And they will be here after us.

That's what people like about the ocean.

Sitting at the desk writing these letters, I know that the questions cannot be answered. I suppose contentment lies in not knowing. The conclusion is that there is no conclusion. I surf this moment, with the wind from the Atlantic battering the window pane.

And as for you, well, nobody will ever know.

I don't know you anymore. But I long for you. I sometimes meet you on the street and feel we have met before. Sometimes I think you are a stranger, and then I recognise you with my heart.

I call you beloved. But in the end that's only me trying to put my words on the mystery of you.

I am only here for a short while, my heart whispers. What happened in Beaumont cannot compare to the waves. This little life of mine is as a drop in that same ocean.

Going out of the house, I am reaching towards the ocean with my eyes even as I lock the door behind me. I am already gone to the sea, and the dry sand and the grassy dunes.

One day I stopped in the car park and had a cheese and bacon sandwich from the van that sold crepes and other delicious foods.

One day I met a woman who was full of anxiety. But I didn't know why.

And one day I met a man who was sitting on one of the benches overlooking the strand. And he had so much longing in his face that he could barely speak to me. But he didn't explain himself either.

He was enthralled to the sea. He was having a different kind of conversation.

And the longing goes on. And the sea is wounded.

November 2021

I love the month of the dead. The washing away of the
year in withering leaves and unrelenting storms and
dark nights and talk of ghosts.

My company of holy souls were still in the house
haunting me; I was still in Donegal, alone, saying
farewell to the year. In the previous 12 months I had
been in Beaumont twice. I wanted to remember it, and
bid it farewell.

I recall a lot of fuss around my bed the night
before and the morning of my operation. Before the
procedure various people attended me to take blood
samples, check my heartbeat and shine lights in my
eyes. They asked my date of birth over and over again.
They instructed me to put on a tiny gown as short as

a miniskirt with tie strings at the back and stockings so tight that it took two nurses to get them on to my big feet.

'Do I get high heels as well?' I wondered, but they explained that the stockings would prevent blood clots. And that put the smile on the other side of my face.

As they wheeled me down the corridor, in and out of various elevators, I watched fluorescent lights on the ceilings passing over me like the light of angels.

Closer to the theatre suites a doctor approached in full green gown, mask and cap, and read me a litany of things that could go wrong with a high-tech spinal procedure.

They swung me from the trolley to an operating table and manoeuvred my head into some kind of plastic brace and I saw various screens floating above me and a nozzle of oxygen coming towards me just as I went unconscious.

I had been reading *The Road to Unfreedom* by Timothy Snyder during the previous week about the dark practices of Vladimir Putin and so in my dreams Putin appeared as a doctor with a syringe leaning over me. He spoke Russian but I told him he had the wrong patient.

Then I woke up in a high-dependency ward and all the people around me were snoring. It was after midnight.

During the following days, a dark-haired woman from Romania lay in the bed next to mine. She spent hours on the phone to her family. She propped the phone against a dinner plate when she was eating or else she'd lie on her back with the phone on the pillow. Her laughter was so reassuring as she chatted with her children that I realised her presence was helping me to heal faster.

After a few days I was moved to a room full of men, which didn't impress me; being stuck day and night with other males felt about as attractive as being incarcerated in the gorilla enclosure at Dublin Zoo. But, in fact, the men also helped me to heal faster.

They talked about divorce, renovating houses, working out in the gym and most especially about their motorbikes. Some of them needed painkillers at night but yet they were cheerful, and grateful for every morsel of food and medicine they received. Their collective chatter shielded me from self-pity and reminded me that being human is the accomplishment of a group rather than an individual.

Apart from the cheerfulness of other patients, it is mainly the staff in any hospital who bring about healing: taking bloods, distributing tablets, serving breakfasts, cleaning floors and closing the curtains, sometimes in the afternoons, so that the wounded world can rest.

The co-ordinated fabric of their care makes a hospital feel as busy as a train station betimes, but underlying each meticulous intimacy with the bodies of strangers is a quality of compassion that is the mark of their humanity.

One day I overheard two nurses discussing a coffee break at the foot of my bed.

'You take the first break,' one of them said. 'You look tired.'

'No,' the second one said. 'It's just that I got no sleep last night.'

Maybe she had just moved house and was worried about the mortgage. Maybe she had a sick child at home. Maybe she was pregnant. Anything is possible. Because every hospital worker has their own story, their own worries and struggles. It's just that they forget themselves so completely when they're on duty, that nobody notices.

And I never found out what her story was because I was discharged the following day. But I think about her a lot. I think about all of them with an enormous sense of gratitude.

To an Old School Friend

I miss the cats. I swear to Jesus it's the one thing I miss from Leitrim when I'm away.

You just can't have a cat in Donegal. It wouldn't be right. Before all this catastrophe regarding my health I was snug as a bug in Leitrim tracking Trump on CNN in between conversations with the cat.

Together we watched Trump every day. Charlie the big black tom straddled my lap with such serenity that I wondered might Trump not benefit from being reincarnated as a cat. Although the thought of a marmalade Trump replete with an orange tail and whiskers exuding toxic emotions while sitting on my lap was a terrifying prospect. And I'd hate to imagine what Trump might do with a mouse.

Not that Charlie my black tom is tolerant of mice. He used to treat them with the same sadistic pleasure as any member of his species. And he was cantankerous at times, especially when his dinner was late or if he was forced to wait outside the door too long in the mornings. But except when he yawned, he was a great companion during the lockdowns.

There I was in Leitrim with trees outside the window losing more leaf every day. In the distance I could see my neighbours' chimneys wheezing smoke. They too had cats. They too waited for Covid to go. We waited for two years, watching the leaves come and go, bloom and die, because we had no choice but to shelter indoors and let the sitka woods grow tall.

That's what it was like before Beaumont.

But after Beaumont, Covid seemed to be dissipating and I came to the coast to recuperate, where the ocean reflects light onto every headland and cliff. And I'm here still, seven months later, although I can't bear the fact that I abandoned the cats in Leitrim.

You see, a cat wouldn't survive here. Young men drive so fast around the roads that any tabby with intelligence would never come out from under the chair in the kitchen. And the house I'm staying in is close to the road.

In fact when I came first, I remarked as I drove around the place that there wasn't a cat to be seen anywhere. I asked a man in Croithlí one day about this and he said there were plenty of cats but that it was too windy for them to be outside.

Which sounded plausible. And since Donegal men are always outdoors, it only makes sense that the cats would remain indoors.

But he said there might be another reason why the cats stay close to the fire in Donegal.

'What's that?' I wondered.

'Well,' he said, 'it might be too noisy for them to be outdoors.'

'Go on.'

'Donegal men enjoy the outdoor life so much,' he said, 'that on a clear day the lawnmowers around the hills kick up a terrible ruction. Like a swarm of bees in the wind. And they shave their lawns as smooth as billiard tables.'

After that I began noticing the lawns. The tight cut on grass from Bloody Foreland to Burtonport. And in one filling station I even saw a toy lawnmower for sale. I've seen toy tractors, toy cars, and even toy fire brigades, but toy lawnmowers was a new one on me. So the children are groomed into the joy of clean lawns from an early age and outdoor cats would need headphones if they wanted to have a sleep on any porch or doorstep.

So while I'm here in seclusion, the cats are sitting cosy in Leitrim where the lady wife attends to their every need.

Peabody was a wild beast when I met him first. He was never in a house in his life. I think perhaps he comes from a long lineage of wild cats. His fur is so coarse that a brush wouldn't go through it even if he let you touch him. And as the years went on he went blind and deaf, and relied on Charlie the black tom to guide him everywhere. And then Peabody eventually after five or six years was lured into the house, with his own basket. They sleep like little bees in a flower. They groom each other. They play and wrestle and chase birds together. The two of them at night in the scullery would gladden your heart, their happy faces looking up as if to say thanks for supper and see you in the morning.

Peabody has become the calm buddha, sitting all day without the slightest bit of bother. While poor Charlie has become increasingly anxious, neurotic, and now we think he has cancer.

He vomits all the time. His fur has turned from black silk to a matt brown. His legs are thin and the skin on his shoulders is developing bald patches.

My beloved was taking him to the vet one morning and, trying to be helpful, I suggested that if it was time to put him down, I would be happy to take care of it. Not meaning that I would stuff him in a bag with stones and throw him in the lake as people used to do when I was a child, but that I would take him to the vet, and be the one to hold him in my arms as he fell asleep.

The beloved looked like she had been hit by a strong bolt. She was horrified.

I protested that people nowadays are getting used to the idea of assisted dying for humans so what's so terrible in saying that I would be glad to step in and assist Charlie to die if it was a better alternative to letting him suffer for months with cancer.

She said nothing and we dined in silence.

But now I'm up here in Donegal and I regret terribly saying such a thing. Not just that she thought so little of me for the ruthlessness of my offer, but guilty in my own soul that I would think of doing it to Charlie.

When I had a near nervous breakdown in 2015, when my depression got so bad that I booked a Ryanair flight and then on the day of the flight couldn't come out of my room, never mind go to Dublin and get on the plane, it was Charlie who rescued me; he came to me every night and scratched at the door, and his pleading would draw me out to the sunroom and I'd sit on the sofa with him and pet him as the tears came down my face. He was my friend and he was encouraging me to get well.

I loved him for that. I loved him too when after the first operation in Beaumont, which didn't work, and I was lying at home with a paralysed gut, barely able to move my body at all around the room, he would come and massage my stomach.

Every evening he did it; he came in the sliding doors, and he'd massage me for about half an hour and then abruptly go off for his supper in the kitchen. I became convinced that he knew there was something wrong with my body and he was trying to heal it. And it helped me hugely in an emotional way to cope with the horror of that winter, before I returned to Beaumont for the second operation which, thank God, seems to have worked splendidly.

So here I am, alone in Donegal, thinking about him. Thinking of all the love he gave me. How like a mother he was to me in times of sickness. And how horrified my beloved was when she saw how quick I was to consider ending his existence without any ado.

It's even worse than what happened with Brambles.

Brambles was a pony we bought in Drumshanbo mart when the child was small, and we kept the pony in a shed at the back of the house.

I went to Paris for a few months and when I came back the place was all messed up. The garden was mud, and there were bales of straw and hay all over the place, so I took Brambles to the mart and got rid of him. All done before I quite understood the trauma this might cause for the rest of the household. Because the child loved Brambles dearly. And nobody asked her was it okay if I disposed of him so suddenly. It was perhaps the most horrible act I'd ever committed. But putting my hand up with enthusiasm to assist in terminating the cat was even worse; Brambles had only been in our lives as a family for a matter of months, whereas Charlie was actually part of the family for years. Even to me he had been so much more than a pet; he was a friend when I needed support.

And why am I telling you this? I suppose because here in Donegal I get remorseful and I try to write letters, and ponder some of the times I have let people down. But it would never be complete if I didn't acknowledge that my track record with other sentient beings is not so wonderful either. And I can't write to Charlie. Cos he can't read. And Peabody is blind. So there's only you, my friend.

And that's my story.

Hope you're having a good day.

PS: Is it men or what? Like maybe we have a straight-line kind of thinking, which combines with self-preservation or self-interest and allows us to kill just that bit easier.

Or would women be so lethal? I don't know and I wouldn't dare raise that as a topic of conversation at any dinner table, even if there still were dinner tables where I could go.

Put it this way: when it comes to motherhood, I failed often.

Period.

A tree is the home of the bird and the bee and the insect. But even to me the tree is a mother, embracing me. And it is the same with the sea. She is the great mother; and a home for the whale, and the whale is my brother.

So when the sun rises over the mountain and the clouds grow melancholic in the mid-morning and I am led or dragged to this water, I understand that I am being led, or being dragged, and that I am never in charge.

That's what the waves whisper to me. I am never in charge. Surrender to me and you will find peace. Because heaven can only be found at the feet of the mother. And I say okay, okay, and I walk and walk the endless beach.

To a Priest

Pat O'Brien was a towering intellect, committed to a radical vision of a Christian Church, a friend of Dan Berrigan, a poet and philosopher, and most of all a devout parish priest in the West of Ireland for many decades.

Pat,

Of all the dead, you are the one I will miss the most. When John O'Donohue died I missed him too, but now it's you, and this is worse because the bodies are being piled up. The graveyards are filling. The tragedies are heaped one on top of another.

How many times did you and I sit in various rooms and discuss O'Donohue? How many times did John and I sit in other rooms and discuss you? And how many times did both of you sit in the same room and discuss my hopes and dreams?

We were about each other. We belonged to each other.

We realised that our lives were intertwined in such a deep way, each of us holding enormous misgivings about the Christian Church, each of us burning to create something beautiful either in poetry or prose, and each of us still unable to shake off that sense of transcendence that glimmers in every flower. Unable to wake from the dream of God with us.

They say that such dreams are delusional, masculine and toxic. They say that the history of humanity is the history of power relationships and oppression.

And to be honest, it's difficult not to be persuaded by such a view.

But we stood on different ground. Unnamable ground.

We clung to a faith that said there was neither male nor female and that all was one in the one God. We said that there was male and female and together the polarity of it, the yin and yang of it, was an exquisite mathematics that somehow reflected God. We said that male and female made a single icon of God's presence. We held the absurd belief that God became human. That God was closer to us than our jugular vein.

Of course that's not what bound us together. It was rather the unease we had as seminarians that we were in the wrong boat. It was a shallowness in us when we presumed we were in the right boat.

It was as if we knew that nailing our colours to the mast was a mistake. We knew we were in the wrong place at the wrong time. We held to an odd realm and our faith was folly and foolishness.

I remember just before you were ordained, we went for dinner together in Dublin and found a teddy bear and sent it anonymously to the papal nuncio in the Phoenix Park. It was a childish undergraduate gesture, but it also made tangible the disaffection we felt with the institution into which we were all about to be ordained.

Secretly we belonged outside. Yet we felt it our burden to follow tradition.

I remember the note we added to the teddy bear. Something about hoping that his eminence would go home to Italy and that if he was idle, then he could play with the teddy.

The gesture had no focus; maybe it was more about trying to declare solidarity between ourselves. We were co-conspirators once the big brown paper bag was delivered across the desk of the post office.

I was the first to cut my stick; abandoning the ministry just four years after ordination, not for any crisis of faith but simply, as I put it to my bishop, because I could make no sense of the celibate life. And 17 years after his ordination John left. Wrenched himself away from all that ritual he loved, to become a writer, renowned across the world. He went so high and so suddenly that the world finally realised what we had seen all along: his eloquence and intellectual prowess.

We had seen it regularly in small seminars and workshops and study groups in college, and what we saw so often in residential rooms in the seminary, or in the drawing rooms of little curacies in Galway or Mayo, when John was in full flight, synthesising Hegelian philosophy with Christian ethics or just handling enormous ideas like the influence of Marxism on Russia with the same lightness as if talking about a local football team.

It won't last, he would say, offhandedly, back in the eighties, about the Soviet system. It was a time when Irish artists were heading for holidays in Cuba, Libya or whatever socialist state sounded close enough to the Soviets to be fashionable. It was a time when Irish writers were heading for Russia to give readings, and wearing badges with the Soviet flag on their lapel. We were certainly oddballs to be still stuck in the Catholic clerical system, but to be fair, it was also a time when people like the poet Irina Ratushinskaya was still trying to write her poems with a splinter of wood on the back of a bar of soap as she lingered in a Soviet camp in Siberia.

The real oppression, many Irish artists and writers declared, was in the West. And the Church was the real oppressor.

O'Donohue saw it differently. Russia will shake off all that Soviet stuff, he said. Russian people are far too spiritual to weather Marxism much longer, he said.

And I could only listen and whisper, 'I hope so.'

And you would nod and shove the spectacles back up your nose and take a long inhalation from a cigarette. And I would just be glad I was hanging out with both of you because I felt like the wooden stick among the incense sticks. If I stayed close to you both for long enough something might rub off on me.

John was right about everything and it's no wonder he went so high like a shooting star and lit up the night sky and dazzled the world. My regret was that I didn't keep in touch with him. That I didn't make the effort to contact him on so many occasions. And when I met him on that day in Galway, as he came out of Kenny's and I said hello and then passed on, my deep regret is that I did not stop and say, 'John, I really miss you.'

Not that I was any better a friend to you. After finding me a place to stay in Galway when my life in theatre wasn't going very well and I had no money, and I suppose I had made all the wrong career moves.

It was a good lesson regarding the shallow nature of the artistic life and perhaps the first time I realised that art was better understood not as a career but simply the tracks of the animal. If one had a life, if one lived a life well, then the tracks might be okay. That path could be called artistic.

You were at my ordination. You arrived an hour before the gig on a motorbike and stayed for days, falling in love with strangers and reciting poetry for anyone who would listen.

There were times I wondered would you leave the ministry. The entire country sometimes seemed to be wondering if you'd leave.

But you stayed. You lingered, some would say, and you conducted the wedding ceremony for myself and my beloved. And that was the end of it. That was the point at which we drifted apart.

Sometimes people would ask me, 'How is Pat O'Brien?'

And I would say, nonchalantly, that I wasn't in contact with you much.

I had a haughty way of saying it. As if I couldn't be bothered. As if by leaving the ministry I had reached a higher level of knowing beyond where you were still stuck. And how ashamed I am of that now.

But living with God's invisible presence in everything was a simple truth for you; it was about routines like saying mass, celebrating that ritual every day, no matter how bad you felt. It was always the chance to begin again each morning and try better. That, I think, is what kept you going. You stayed because you were the sinner. We left with the outrageous arrogance of supposing that we never sinned.

I wanted to finish the paragraph. I was rushing the words because I needed to get out again and walk, before it rained.

People saw the anti-nuclear stuff you were involved with as some kind of liberation theology. Bishops were afraid of you, thinking you were a radical. Whatever that means. But far from being a Marxist, you ended up as the country priest.

Walking on the road inland towards Croithlí, I notice
that there are ash trees in Donegal with berries as red
as fresh blood and I was curious as to why the berries
had not been eaten. In Leitrim the birds are ravenous.
When berries grow heavy in bunches on the ash tree
the starlings and thrushes and smaller birds take each
tree on a particular day, fleecing it of all fruit. But not
so, apparently, here in Donegal.

The red berries here are hanging heavy even though
it's November.

I phoned you on the 6th of August. It was a lovely day at the
beach and I got a box of fruit from a friend on the same day.
A man much younger than myself whom I'd taught years
ago in secondary school. Your birthday was in early August
too and for a few years after we lost contact I used to call
you in August to say hello, and check up on how things were
in your priestly ministry over in the West. How you were
getting on with all your literary adventures, corresponding
with Dan Berrigan and Denise Levertov and Seamus Heaney
and writing poems and haunting the bookshops in Galway.

You mentioned you were having health problems. I asked
for details.

'Cancer,' you said.

It floated in the air for a while; like a black balloon. I wondered would the wind blow it away. I didn't want to go further. I didn't want to ask where or how much or how bad it was, or would you get better.

'Do you remember when Reagan came to Galway? And you were in the forefront of the protests, releasing black balloons over the city when he was driving through. That was a beautiful act of protest.'

I don't know why I said that on the phone. Maybe I found it difficult to think of something appropriate. You mentioned your cancer. So I jumped into a memory of the past when you were at your most heroic. But the fact is that there was no flow of words between us.

'So,' I said, 'I'll write to you soon.' That's what I said. I'm nearly sure I promised to write. Four months ago. Four months before you died. And now here I am, putting pen to paper when it's too late.

My letter was gone off the cliff. There was something about his death that I couldn't accept. The full moon lit up the waves and the apron of sand stretched before me like a ballroom of ghosts. Rocks in the distance might be human figures gone beyond the grave. This ocean might be a portal to a deeper level of being and the beach might be full of people who are no longer visible.

Later I tried, by moonlight, with a small lamp over the writing desk, to begin again. Because Pat was still imposing a strong presence on my mind. He was an owl that haunted the house until dawn, smoking Major cigarettes and drinking Black Bush whiskey and sometimes when he was reading in one corner and I in the other, I could hear his breath. He had a distinctive way of catching his breath. People have things like that; little idiosyncrasies that can identify their breathing as singularly as a fingerprint. And so I sat up that night alone in the house, trying to write like I was speaking to him, and the wind from the Atlantic pushed at the window and the hall door, and when he wasn't in the room with me I could hear him mooching about on the corridor or in the attic.

What I couldn't understand was your melancholy. It was as if the holocaust was constantly tormenting you. The struggles of de Beauvoir and Sartre and Dostoyevsky were as intimate to you as family squabbles. And I could never get to your heart. I could never find where the place was that your own heart struggled. It was always about the others. About the heroes and the great intellectuals of history. And you gathered their issues and made them your own.

I'd watch you in the kitchen of your parochial house in Skehana, with a mug of tea and a cigarette at the kitchen table early in the morning, looking out the window, waiting on the postman to bring you a new book of poetry. But I felt there was something you weren't telling me. I wondered was there something you weren't telling anyone.

And if I had opened that door for you, we might have had an even richer friendship. Ever so slightly I saw you as a saint, a crucified mind, who understood the agony of the cross more than others. As if you had penetrated the mystery of incarnation and you could see how terrible the beauty was, how tragic the risen Christ was, how awful the pit that we end up in can be, and how even Christ cannot take away the destiny we face in the grave; all he can do is guide us into it and through it.

All this frightens me as I get older. I wish I still had you beside me. Maybe we could figure out the conundrum of the risen Christ. How the Christian message is pointless if it doesn't mean the body is transformed. Maybe not the gross body that the Buddhists talk about, and maybe not even the subtle body that might be akin to a Western idea of a soul, but the enlightened glorious dharma body; the transformed being beyond all personal life that shines in the ground of being and in whom the ground of being finds a lens.

A human lens. God not in the godhead but in the vulnerable, broken, wounded body. God in the sick and withering body. Could we not have had more time talking about those things?

And why is it that all the men in 4,000 years of holy scriptures always go out to find God. They go to deserts, mountain peaks, far-off countries, and they cross oceans, all to find him. And if they do, he is always at a distance, in the bush or the cloud or the little invisible breath of wind that comes when there is no wind.

But women, on the other hand, in those same scriptures are invariably found by God. They don't go looking. It's God that comes to say hello, by means of an angel, a gift, a whisper or just the beautiful man standing at the well, waiting for her to arrive with a bucket so that he can speak with her.

Why is that? And could we not have had more time to talk about it?

The wind died down and I could no longer hear his breath and no longer sense his footfall at the door. Pat O'Brien. He was not there. The house was empty. And yet in the emptiness I felt his answer. I sensed his smile in the darkness.

There's no point, in the end, to all this talk. Naming the bird and ceasing to hear the song. Allowing the mind to be riddled with convictions, axioms, principles and theological truths.

As Aquinas said, it's all straw. And there is only one thing required.

So I sat for a long time at the window, with the stillness of night, and the moon falling into the Atlantic.

'It's lovely to hear your voice,' you whispered. 'That was so intimate. It made me feel good. It was like being touched.'

Because it felt like my voice was touching you, reaching out to you in your hospital bed in Galway. And the other thing about it was, your own voice was so familiar. Everything was said in that last phone call.

Where were you when I called?

I was coming.

How long were you there?

Years.

Where?

Outside your door.

Are you afraid?

I can remember turning away before.

Did you speak of the moon?

I spoke of history.

You must always speak of the moon. That's the only way we get out of here.

You were a shaman in the face of death's great annihilation. And priesthood was your trade. I could hear the ventilator in the background. I could imagine you in bed. I am only beginning to understand what loss is. But can you imagine the shock I felt at how familiar your voice was.

It's 40 years since we were ordained.

How quickly the church collapsed.

How fast I fled, just four years in ministry. How courageously you endured, faithfully serving as a parish priest for all those decades, despite the scandals and the outrage and the madness of mandarins in the Vatican who would polish the pyramids with their toothbrushes faster than they would manage to reform the creaking monolith of their imperial institution.

I remember calling you from Cork on your thirtieth birthday. I knew it because it fell in August two days after my own.

The brightest intellectual star of them all, on the side of non-violence, and introducing us all to Thomas Merton as a great hope for the Church at one time when we thought the Church had a future. But at least you remained in the ministry and gave yourself for 40 years to others in the small sacraments of heaven that manifest in ordinary life, as you blessed the newborn and led the coffins of the dead across the rocky island roads to their burial places.

Curiously, you came into my mind around Easter in 2021 when I was in Beaumont hospital. It was 40 years since my own ordination and I was remembering those early days, so innocent and green, trying to cope with old people, because even in those days it was usually old people that a priest would interface with. Anointing the sick, sitting up all night with the dying, and taking communion to the elderly women knitting in the corners of their own kitchens. Old men outside their front doors smoking pipes; taking the bread of heaven into their homes on the first Friday of every month and trying to maintain a sense of the sacred as they talked about a football match the previous Sunday.

That day in Beaumont a chaplain came around and asked me did I want to pray with her, and I said I wanted to talk. She sat by the bed and listened as I went through my stories. I told her how I had been impressed in the early days by people like you, who had vision and passion, and how I'd become disillusioned with the institution after a year or two and tried to plough my own furrow as a dissident. How I'd struggled to embrace modernity but just couldn't live without religious faith. And how I'd turned to Buddhism for decades until at last the accident of an icon, with two big eyes gazing at me from the wall, turned my heart again to the possibility of living in the light of Christ.

She sat by the bed and she too had big eyes and for all I knew was an icon of infinite mercy, a sign of hope on a day when I was emotionally as flat as a pancake.

I said I would pray in my heart and she might do the same for me because I could not bear to share the same words as her. And I knew as she left my bedside that it had been the wrong decision, and that I had made it out of pride. The prayers of the Church had become clichés to me, enfolded in so many presumptions that were politically incorrect. So to say 'Hail Mary' or 'Our Father' seemed impossible.

I could not open my heart in prayer with her for fear I might seem vulnerable. And there I was in a hospital bed with so many things gone wrong with my body. But pride is the last thing to go.

I had intended writing this to you for a while. It's something that happened early on and I never forgot it. I was in a woman's house during Holy Week when the oil of ordination was not yet dry on my hands. This happened 40 years ago when I was a chaplain to a nursing home in Cork. One of the elderly ladies asked me to visit her daughter who lived nearby.

So I did. I ate a piece of tipsy cake in her kitchen on Spy Wednesday. We ate the cake by the kitchen range and looked out on the back yard rain, at three white sheets that flapped and blew and raged.

She left me to go after them before they tore the clothes line down. I watched her struggling with pegs, a mouth full of them, and in wellingtons too big for her. She was barely able for the bundled weight at 59 and she said her husband usually got them in.

She had left them out to dry and thought the clouds would not betray her.

As a cleric I stood outside her world as if it were a mystery more enchanting than God's presence; that she would iron them and make them ready for the bed again where, before he died, her husband, a man of big feet and strong wellingtons, would love her. But the sheets were drenched, and I thought of them as shrouds that would not dry, or from which the women could not rinse the blood.

That's how my imagination at the time often mixed Eros, divine tragedy and my own suppressed emotions.

Coming into the kitchen with her arms full, and her skirt and knees all wet where stalks and thistles had flicked across her path, she bent down and rubbed them as she kicked off the boots. And I realised she could be my mother, this woman full of her little businesses, pottering around an empty house where no one came to visit.

I knew her husband was dead. She told me everything. He had died some weeks before in the hospital and I had promised her mother I would call, because that's a nice thing that curates do.

They share the moment. But her world was beyond me and I was clouded in the arrogance of a language I thought I understood.

Sometimes there's little point in saying anything. The words only inhibit us from touching the reality. Sometimes silence becomes the only music worth paying attention to. But I didn't know that back then.

She was pottering around her house as if her husband might still come and fill his wellingtons. That's when she sat down and offered me the tipsy cake. She was loving her way out of the dark.

But she was sitting where no husband sat, and where no God was present, and where no curate should sit; in a place so full of loss and death that no living thing could comfort her. So in Jewish terms she was doing shiva. She was in a place that has no adequate meaning. It is a ritual that you can do, but not explain. A state where you can only embody grief, not rationalise it. A loss you can only accept in the weight of it, and it was all around her and as black as her sheets were wet.

'The children are all at university,' she said, 'but still I do the usual. Like hoovering and polishing and making up the beds in case one of them might make it for the weekend.'

The sheets she basketed by the door were shrouds, and silence dominated our afternoon.

Her fingers burrowed for clothes pegs and I noticed how arthritis was already gathering on her like fraying on the edges of a photograph.

'I suppose we live eternity, but time betrays us.'

You said that to me one time. You were defending the notion of ritual. The fact that sometimes there are no words, and no bridges of meaning that can contain the mystery of our deepest pain and loss. There are times that only rituals work and allow us embody both the betrayal of time and the hope of eternity.

I understand that now, much better as I get older. Time is our Judas, a man we blame unfairly. But it is time and impermanence that are our ultimate fragility. And like the cocoon, they are the space in which we struggle with the hope of something new to come. They tear us apart so that we are transformed.

On that long-ago day I held my breath and sat silent in her kitchen. I thought that people who have lived their suffering deeply didn't need the effrontery of a shallow boy priest trying to encapsulate the catastrophe of death in sentimental words or prayers.

But I was wrong, and that was the difference between us. You stayed in the Church not for political reasons or for career objectives or because you were in denial about the scandalous leadership that had run the ship onto the rocks.

You stayed because someone must bury the dead, and bless

the newborn. Burying the dead was your trade. Breaking bread and blessing children and old people was your ordinary life.

You wanted to accompany the grief-stricken. To walk in their shoes.

And you served your time in hospital corridors, at sick beds, and at gravesides. You were there in the pouring rain, with the slim purple ribbon around your neck like a tiny scarf, flapping in the wind, and a bottle of holy water in your hand as you skited the coffins and blessed the mourners, and tossed the first handful of clay on the lid. You were faithful in love, not to a church but to other fragile people who needed someone to journey with them, in rituals of hope, and in times of darkness.

When the tipsy cake was finished and the tea gone cold she turned her back on me to wash the dishes. I held my breath as her crooked hands patrolled the crockery and settled down each plate on the drying board.

'You're very quiet,' she said.

And I agreed. But what could I say, on a day of poverty, and empty sheets and rain.

Suffice it that I was there, attending to her rituals of grief. Her ritual of sheets that she took in from the rain and that tomorrow she would try once more to dry and iron and hope that someone came to fill them.

I knew so little about life and was so unconscious in my cosy religious zeal that I felt my cheeks turn red. I thanked her for the cake and fled, making mist rise on the pathway as I ripped up the gravel in my Datsun Cherry. I couldn't stay any longer with her. But you, Pat, you stayed 40 years in those kitchens, sharing that silence.

And 40 years later I found myself struggling through the same Holy Week, the same rituals of Good Friday revolving in my imagination as I resolved to write to you, that day, or maybe the following. Just to write all this to you and suggest we meet. And what then?

What then, Pat?

Where would this conversation have brought us? I wondered, as I waited inside the curtains for the nurse to come and release me from a catheter.

I finished for the night. If it were an email it would be sent. A button pressed and that's the end of it. But there's a real ontological problem with emails. They just don't travel into the metaphysical sphere like old letters.

Letters can lie on a shelf for years until they have yellowed and read differently if you pick them up, like they might have been written in heaven or might contain fresh messages from another dimension. You can savour them on the desk for days as they ripen in their wisdom. I think there is a force in such documents, like sacred scriptures that heal, and evolve through time; it's a language thing. We become the words; and old words become new as we embody them. Every time I take up the pages of old letters they are richer and deeper than they were when I first read them.

Thank you for taking me with you to the island in 1979 when you got your first posting as a curate. I stayed in the house with you for three months. The bath was full of dirty dishes just like in the film *Buddawanny* which had been made the year after you left. The film was a fictional story written by someone else, but the world imagined was yours. Your wild house, with the bathtub of dishes, and the wok you used for exotic meals in the kitchen, and the corridor between the two front rooms where I once saw Professor Tom Marsh collapse. He was in one room and I saw his body lean and fall so that he ended up on the floor with his head in the other room.

Tom was a capable enough drinker but he never reckoned on an afternoon in the house of Michael Joe O'Malley, philosopher, poet and maker of his own whiskies. A few hours with Michael Joe and we were all on the floor. That was just one memorable moment in a wonderful holiday. The best of course for me was the night I went down to the hotel and met a woman from Dublin and never came back until the following morning; one of the best moments in my life.

I had never loved a stranger until then. And loving her was real because in all the years since, I have only grown my affection for her memory. Now in old age I cherish our innocence, as we delighted in each other, the two of us then still in our twenties.

Me and her falling asleep in each other's arms without knowing each other's names. The morning so beautiful with the white walls of the hotel glistening, the room drenched with sunlight, and her perfumes and silk garments all over the place because of the furore we had stirred the night before in our enthusiasm and the sound of the Atlantic outside the window.

But thank you for teaching me about Tolstoy and Dostoyevsky and how to live with poetry. How to revere poets as real human beings, who were only struggling to make sense of the world. For teaching me how to read poetry with compassion. To read it not as truth or words with meaning but as if every verse were a map to nowhere made in desperation by someone wanting to find a path to love.

You embodied the reader of poetry. From the first moment we connected, with a bottle of Black Bush at the bottom of a stairwell in Maynooth. After the pub, on our way back into the labyrinthine world of the seminary, I could see that poetry was the map of your heart.

Paul Durcan's description of you in his long poem, 'Greetings to Our Friends in Brazil' as you both watched the All Ireland Final on television is wonderful. He describes your passion and bewilderment so eloquently that every time I read the poem you are alive to me again. It's a joyful irony that you, who loved poetry as the maps of meaning and the surest path to faith, would be embodied so completely in someone else's poem.

But now you cannot write. You can never write again. You cannot read a poem. You cannot see. You cannot hear. And this letter is far too late. I'm looking at one of the Christmas cards you sent me from Clare Island. It's still on the shelf behind me and might sit there for another decade. And yet you are gone. You cannot enjoy the sun or walk the beach or drive a car or eat the grapes or drink the wine.

I ought to have sent this letter in August, after our phone call.

Forgive me.

I see you still, Pat, on your motorcycle, pushing up the rickety lanes across Clare Island to drink whiskey with that great rustic philosopher with the handlebar moustache, Michael Joe O'Malley. A man who could make his own whiskey, and drink it, sweetly, to garnish the conversation. You were kindred with him. And kindred with the young woman facing death ten years before your own death, and kindred with so many dying. That's what they said about you afterwards.

You were prayerful. You visited the sick. You were close to the dying.

And with you it was always the ritual. Even when you met Áine Ryan on the street in Galway one day you surprised her by rushing over to her on Quay Street and asking her could you give her a blessing. And she agreed and one might wonder if you had a notion that she needed one.

But it was the other way around. It was you who were already seriously ill and you knew it, and you needed to express your love once again with an old friend by giving her what was deepest and most precious to you.

Your blessing.

Just imagine the conversation we could have had; and all the guff that could be said about priests, and celibacy and equality and the official Church's crimes, and where do people go now that there is no Church, and what would Dostoyevsky or even Tarkovsky or Arvo Pärt say to these situations, and all the other stuff we might have talked about over whiskey for years, you and me. Not to mention the darkness of war in Ukraine.

Maybe as a poet you knew more than anyone how love finds its ultimate expression in silence. And in silence we find a path to love.

Which reminds me of Merton. He was your real mentor. Merton the monk, the solitude, the recluse, and Merton the poet of so many books. It was the silence between the words that mattered to him. And to you. And maybe you will forgive me for not writing to you before now. For not contacting you and taking the trouble to arrange an evening when we could have talked one last time. Maybe you will forgive my silence on the phone when we spoke again, a few days before you passed away. When I heard your voice speak, even breathless as it was, and heard your whole life in the sound of it.

The man you were, gathered into a few spoken words. And all you said was my name. And that it was good to hear the sound of my voice. You were clinical sometimes in your sense of truth. Clinically exact.

My voice. Your voice. And the silence in between the few words we had, knowing that this was the last moment we could ever speak in this lifetime. And yet we left so much on that call for the silence to devour.

But maybe that was wise. Maybe at that late stage we both knew it was in silence that everything ends and begins.

So everything was said because nothing was said.

And sometimes I can still hear you and hear your lonely, melancholic silence. Your stoic acceptance of the things that go wrong; and of the cross, the rosary, the holy water and the purple stole. The instruments of your trade.

I will push the poetic strings that hold my world together and hope that you are taking the wine elsewhere now. And hope that you are just beyond my fingertips and present on a different level. You nurtured my mind with great books when we were students. You harboured me for months on an island. You came to my ordination, married me and my beloved in the little church in Skehana 30 years ago, and when you were dying you paid me such an astonishing compliment that I was taken aback.

Ah, says you, it's lovely to hear your voice. But you should have heard it more often, and much sooner as you waited out those last days and weeks with cancer. We only had time to speak for a few minutes because you were impossibly short of breath, the cancer eating your lungs, and the ventilator rasping away in the background all the time.

Perhaps we can discuss it all tomorrow.

With Kazantzakis and Kavifis.

Under the pine and cedar trees.

We can think of peaches. And plums. And why they grow.

The Chinese say they grow for themselves.

They certainly do not grow for you any longer.

DECEMBER 2021

Winter now, short evenings and a slanting light in the sky as I walk behind the sand dunes to avoid the wind. I'm not alone. Not that anyone is here with me. But the emptiness inside has been completed. After enough time, emptiness becomes like a companion. That's how it is in old age.

Longing becomes a chamber in the heart.

I went home for Christmas. I closed up the house in Donegal for a few days and drove to Leitrim.

I went to Carrick on Shannon to buy Christmas decorations, because I wanted to get in the mood, to drench the garden with all that cheap vulgar light I had been resisting for years.

In my Christmas childhood, quiet paper decorations hung from the ceiling in demure curves, like Tibetan prayer flags, lagging from the four corners towards the central lampshade of fogged glass in the living room.

And outside, the world was dark apart from a candle flickering in every window as we made our way into town for midnight mass.

My mother's abhorrence of waste ensured that the decorations lasted my entire childhood, and the tree itself was lit year after year by the same string of bulbs; dainty shades as small as eggcups and as delicate as eggshells. Half of them were broken, but an electrician was consulted in early December to ensure that at least some lights would work on Christmas Eve.

When the first LED lights twinkled like snowflakes on my mother's tree ten years after my father died, I was enormously sad at the loss of our old-fashioned Christmas bulbs. Although over time I grew to admire the digital inventiveness built into Christmas decorations, which nowadays permits places like Mullingar to sparkle in the dark. And I love walking the frozen pavements of Warsaw in December when gigantic gift-wrapped boxes and reindeers bigger than horses are strewn about the pavements, all formed in flashing dots of coloured light.

I still sometimes mourn the loss of my childhood Christmas when everything was imagined in darkness: Santa silently treading along the roof tiles; mother

Mary and her infant hiding in a straw manger beneath the breath of donkeys; and stars, of course, stars on every drumlin around Cavan town.

Nowadays, urban gardens are awash with reindeers, elves and characters from Roald Dahl, and while an orchestra of flashing colours outside the window has its merits, the velvet sensation of pure darkness has completely gone, and light no longer feels like something fragile or impermanent.

At Christmas time I found myself packing the Corolla with boxes of battery-driven decorations in the half-light of a shopping centre car park, wondering what they would look like hanging from the trees.

There was no meaning or method in my arrangement of them later; I simply scattered everything on random branches. I strung a long, red rope of light across the bones of a bare ash tree, and wound a soft amber cluster of dots around a maple. I positioned three projectors on the grass to shine laser red dots on beech trees in the woodland. And finally I plastered the wall of the house with a dappled light that mimicked the fall of snow, and I drenched the hedge with Santa hats. It was gaudy and garish and vulgar, and I loved it like a child.

That evening the temperature in Leitrim went down to minus 2 and the sky was so clear and the ground so frosty that it felt like I was in Warsaw once again. When I was finished I pulled off my wellies at the door and sat by the stove with a glass of Drumshanbo whiskey, marvelling at the loudness of the light.

But I read in their gaudy luminosity the same metaphor as sang out from the candle that once stood in the window of every country house long ago, when emigration deprived so many mothers of a Christmas hug, and orphans watched from the windows of many convent buildings across the snow-covered fields wondering why their mothers had vanished into the air. I had been in Tuam to visit the site where the remains of 796 children were buried without ceremony in a sewage system and left unremembered and forgotten for half a century.

I found it easy to celebrate the festival of winter with garish lights and roasted chestnuts and Christmas pudding. But perhaps for the first time in my life there was a hollowness at the core of it. I could not find Christ under the Christmas tree or in the crib. I could not find him anywhere.

Not until after Stephen's Day, when I returned

to Donegal and closed the door again on everything except the sound of the ocean, which seemed to have invaded the house on the storm-blown winter nights at the end of the month.

That's when I found him again.

To the Baby with the Blue Shoe

I can find nobody else to write to on this winter's night. Nobody that might accept my rage. Although it is an affront for me to address you, little angel. You died so young. And your body lies in a sewage system beneath a playground in the town of Tuam. I know because I stood there, on the ground above you. It was at a gathering in the summertime. It was one of the few moments when I dragged myself away from the ocean, because Catherine Corless had asked me to come. She asked me to say something.

And what could I say but address you directly. I had read of your existence in her book, as she described some of the work the archaeologists had done at the site. She said someone had looked in through the fencing that cordoned off the dig, and they'd seen a hole, and down below in the hole they'd seen the bodies.

Bodies of children piled on top of each other. And they were all wrapped in swaddling clothes, but one in particular wore a blue shoe.

A blue shoe, I thought; on the bones of a dead child? Does that mean you were a little boy baby? At least that's a start. Although it may never be known who you were unless they reclaim every single bone and test them for DNA. Only then could someone discover that you were their aunt or uncle and your remains could be reinterred with the appropriate blessings and bells, and with incense and candle light.

I'm writing to you because the veil between this life and eternity is only a veil from our point of view. They say that if you walk towards God then he will run towards you. They say that the visible world we inhabit at the surface is only a surface and that in the depth of our being we endure beyond time or space. That's about the best way I can describe my faith.

That Mary at the tomb of her beloved Jesus awakened to the insight that he was beside her as Christ, and that the triumph of humanity in the dark night of Good Friday came as she saw the light of dawn.

She had journeyed with him for years. She had been loyal at his trial. She had been along the way of sorrow with him and up the hill to where they crucified him. She went with his body shrouded in white to the burial tomb that a friend provided.

She waited there. She watched. She slept. She dreamed. She woke and saw him raised, and glorified and made whole again. How amazing that she saw him bodily. That her heart knew the necessity of embodiment.

All she needed was an empty tomb to open her eyes. And with all her love she saw not her human beloved, but the risen glorified Christ he had become for her. All Earth and life redeemed by the opening that was made in history in that moment, like the tearing of a veil, whereby we leave the surface and see in the depth of things.

God didn't wait for Nietzsche to kill him off.

God died in that moment of insight. God was no longer majestic or imperial, full of power and might, but had become reformed as the wounded victim, the human beloved that had been torn asunder as a criminal.

She saw what no philosopher had imagined or expected, what no previous religious tradition had grasped: she saw that God was not God. That the mould of divinity was what shattered on the cross. And that this human had been raised up in glory.

And only she knew how human he was. How loving he was. How the two were made one in this new thing; God becoming human. God abandoning himself to be remade as human.

Not much has moved forward since then. Not even Dostoyevsky as he put his pen to paper could do better.

Her moment was so intense, so fused with the trauma of watching him suffer and die, and with dreaming him in her sleep, and with experiencing the light of a new day, that it is difficult to ever unwind it, or forget that humanity from then until the end of time will walk in the light of that transformation.

Forgive me for declaring my wonder and awe at the story of Mary Magdalene. It's a love story like no other. But I daresay your mother, while she was incarcerated in the Tuam Mother and Baby Home, didn't spend her time obsessing on tales of exotic love.

Your mother had far too much more to do, thinking about you, and how you might be born, and how that would happen and praying it would go well.

And afterwards, she had too much scrubbing to do, cleaning floors and wiping down the toilets, until her time was up and you were one year old, and she was put out on the road without you.

I wonder did she knock on the gates for years wondering if you were still inside. Or did she go to England and forget you? Did she try to keep some shred of you alive in her heart?

Perhaps the other shoe remained with her. Hidden in the suitcase on the boat to Holyhead. A comrade to the little blue shoe that was still strapped to the bones of your foot when the excavations began in Tuam all those years later. But I suspect she wasn't concerned about theology or the finer points of Mary Magdalene's Christological vision.

Mary Magdalene was a wise and holy woman. It's amazing that after 2,000 years the institutional Church still puts things about her upside down. It astonishes me that anyone would have the gall to incarcerate young women and punish them for nothing more than the love they embodied, and then call the institution of their incarceration a Magdalene laundry.

And I fancy your mother was a holy woman in her own way too. As were they all. Some of their suffering must have been so unbearable that drink and drugs and failed relationships occasionally became the footprint of their lives, and the inevitable consequences of their trauma.

But whereas Mary Magdalene got to bury her Christ your mother was not so lucky. Because the zealots in their pious habits chose to dump the body of her child in the bowels of an old sewage system, without the blessings of bell or candle, and without the comfort of hymn or incense.

The empty tomb told Magdalene that a kind of transformation had occurred, an ontological shift in the nature of this broken body, and that as sure as the tomb was empty her dearest Jesus had been raised in light and truth to become the Christ of all the cosmos. The compassion of the universe whispering the triumph even in her ear as he spoke her name.

So too the sewage system beneath the car park and playground in the town of Tuam, holding so many tiny bodies for so long, cries out to the world now, that there can be no resurrection at the end of time unless and until those children of God are raised up again, and interred with dignity, and acknowledged as radiant in the light of Heaven.

You know nothing of life because you did not live it, and if you could reach me from where you are, then you might not forgive me because I confess I was in thrall to that holy place and all those holy objects.

The sanctuary. The tabernacle. The blessed sacrament. When all the while you were lying there, decade after decade, from the day I was born. Perhaps you were even born the same year. Perhaps your flesh was just as soft as mine as my own mother bathed me and your young mother drenched you with tears in the bath, knowing she would have but one year with you and then forever without you.

I don't know yet how you died. Perhaps we will in time find out when your body is returned to the open sky for the first time after so many years. Perhaps I will be alive to see you brought up from that crypt below the tarmac. The tabernacle of your presence beneath the street. To see your little bones again, raised up like the real presence, the risen Christ in a blue shoe.

A little body over which no one said a funeral mass. Over which no one spread incense or prayed the words of the last farewell – may the angels lead you into Paradise – and yet a little body that someone hugged and loved.

There was no little white coffin to be carried shoulder-high from the church to the grave. Because there was no ritual or ceremony for you. No decade of the rosary was ever said at your grave. And you remain asleep, under the feet of other children who played in that playground for decades.

But nobody knew you were there.

The bishops in their palaces and the nuns in their parlours who manage the Church have unfinished business in that place. They have unfinished business with God. They need to go to that place, raise your body from the earth and acknowledge in you the face of the infant Christ. They need to do their duty and say their prayers and give you the dignified burial that is your due.

Nothing could fly in the face of God's love more than what was done in that house of the dead. The God born as human was disposed of here, in a sewage chamber, secretly, and without blessing or farewell.

I beg for forgiveness. Because like thousands of others, I sat in an armchair and watched the Tuam babies saga play out on television. Then I forgot. As if it had nothing to do with me. Yet I am Christian, and this happened in my name.

Please, someone, please!

Bury them with dignity!

Is that too much to ask?

We do it for our war dead in the midst of battle though the air be thick with smoke and bullets. And we do it for dogs. But these bodies, lying unmarked in the ground beneath our feet, are not dogs. They are human remains.

Blessed are the poor in spirit, for theirs is the kingdom of heaven.
Blessed are they that mourn, for they shall be comforted.

JANUARY 2022

The year turned and the storms came. I could hear them at night. And I resolved not to write to the dead again. I went to the beach but some days it was impossible. The wind whipped up the sand and slapped my cheeks.

I stayed indoors. I watched television. I lit candles before the icons and kept the electric light off so that the golden halos around the icons of the great mother of God and the icon of Christ glowed and warmed me more than any fire.

And there was something sweet about the winter

silence, the winter darkness, the windswept beach and the fast-moving banks of grey cloud that swept across the house touching the roof, hiding the mountains, and making it impossible to drive without wipers or lights.

Some mornings I would write all day because often my younger self on the beach waited for me and I was afraid to go there. The child I once was, in swimming togs, with a bucket and spade, sitting in the sand.

I headed up the hills beyond Croithlí and walked the mountain paths around the lake. Found an old galvanised church and stepped inside. Mooched around the ruins of a schoolhouse.

Men on enormous tractors passed by and watched me. What is he doing in the church at this hour of the morning? they might ask.

Perhaps he is robbing something. They looked like they were remembering my face. Like they would remember it if the police called on them later.

But I waved back, reaching up into the sky, making sure they saw me, and assuring them that I was okay. I know what they were thinking.

And when I failed on the beach, and then failed on

the mountain, I went on to the supermarket for milk
and ten euro of meat and veg.

I hated coming home without milk.

I lock the door and sit looking out the window, and
then sleep becomes my refuge. I am hibernating until
the sun returns.

I can't write again, until it begins again.

To Alice

Alice was an elderly lady I knew in Glangevlin in the 1970s. The parish priest at the time, Eamonn Lynch, showed her great kindness, and wanted to accommodate her in the parish house, but she refused. He offered her various options, but she refused to be separated from her cow, so that she was sometimes lodged in an outhouse in the back yard and spent her days in the kitchen, until a prefab, a one-room space, was built for her. And because I sometimes enjoyed Eamonn's company I too was blessed with her friendship. She had a deep and extraordinary connection with nature and animals, with the rain and sun, and with the dawn and the moonlit nights. Her sense of belonging in the wild world with bees and birds and farming animals embodied a joy that there is no word to describe.

How could I forget you? You were the only one who saw me as a rogue. With one fogged-up eye and one clear eye, you would look at me warily, as you sat on the ditch.

'Hairy Harding,' you'd say, because of my beard. 'Here comes Hairy Harding.'

Other days you wouldn't recognise me even when I sat down beside you.

'Who's there?' you would say.

And when I spoke you'd confess, 'I can't see today.'

And I'd say, 'You can see well enough, Alice. Because the only blindness is in the heart.'

Sitting on the ditch all day with your cow on a rope as she ate from the long acre.

And then one day recently who comes to call on me in Leitrim when I'm not at home but Vincent McGovern, who works in London now and has written a book and wanted to leave it with me. He didn't know I had fled to the sea.

He came all the way from London on a big motorcycle, and I wasn't at home because I'm here in Donegal, but he left the book anyway, and he signed it.

'From Vincent. To Hairy Harding.'

And the phrase took me back to Glangevlin, that beautiful valley in the Cuilce mountains where you and I first met and where you first put that tag on me. The fair valley that gathered in its soul a mythic tale of origins, and a tribe of

McGovern people, and spoke in Gaelic up to the time that you were born.

Hairy Harding was a tag that Vincent and other school-children picked up, and it travelled as a nickname to the adults and all around the valley.

I became almost as renowned as yourself. People would say, 'I seen Hairy Harding and Alice the Goat sitting on the ditch at the church today. What would them two be talking about?'

Indeed. What would you and me be talking about!

But you and I know that we had lots to talk about.

The priest, that kind man Eamonn, who gave both of us lodgings back then, said it first. I remember you were sitting in his kitchen one day, that enormous old kitchen in the priest's house, and he was beside you on the old sofa and you were crying, as you often did, about Rabbit the cow because you were always troubled if Rabbit the cow was coughing too much and maybe would die. Rabbit was like a child to you. She was more than a child. She was husband and wife, mother and father, land and identity; you carried your nation in that cow. You retained your dignity on the roads with that cow.

You had a cow.

'But Alice,' Eamonn said, 'Rabbit is as healthy as a trout.'

I looked at him, wanting to say, *Eamonn, that's too many animals; the cow called Rabbit being as healthy as a trout,* but I said nothing because you were weeping.

You were tiny. You were no more than the height of my waist, and you had long white hair and the old coat tied with rope around your rotund waist.

And you could hardly see because of that foggy eye.

I know what it was now. It was cataracts. Because I had four months of them myself, after my retina detached. But there were no skilled surgeons in those days to fix the eye of a poor woman.

There were no doctors to examine you, except for old Doctor Hawkins in Blacklion with his leather bag and his white hair and of whom you said, 'He's as old as myself,' when you were dismissing the idea of Father Eamonn bringing you down to him for an examination. As if being old implied that he might not have had any schooling.

But Eamonn was kind, and he looked at you weeping over the cow that evening and he said, 'Alice, Rabbit will be well. She can't get sick.'

'Why not?' you wondered.

'Because she has an angel to watch over her,' he said.

And you cried. That's when you cried. Because it was a soft thing to say. A kind thing to say.

'Alice,' Eamonn said, 'you are the angel.'

And later when you were gone out to sleep in the shed, myself and Eamonn reflected on your angelic root, as we sipped mugs of tea.

Truly there was something about you that he had named. There was something of the face of God that he saw. In Islam they say, 'I look everywhere and see the face of God.'

And we looked at you, Alice and saw a light under the skin, a glow of something beautiful, a trace of divine grace. There was something of the angel's voice that I always heard whenever you spoke in that soft Dowra accent.

Eamonn would certainly have given you the softest of blankets if you had agreed to take up residence in that cosy room just off the kitchen. And you would have been the queen of the house. A house built with funding from an American senator in 1927 as a gift to the little mountain parish in Ireland where his people came from. And Eamonn would have been delighted with you there, instead of out in the shed, with a brown cow in one corner and you lying on bales of straw in the other.

At night when I would be coming home from the pub

I'd often hear you talking away to your pet, laughing and sharing jokes, and what I thought strange was the fact that you were never lonely.

'She's an angel,' Eamonn said, in all sincerity.

Because you were giving us so much. Your gentle manners, your alert presence in the room, your quiet-spoken wisdom, came to us like revelations of how to behave in the world.

And you had been through hardship that we could only read about in books.

You were born in a world where your parents were still paying rent in Cavan to Trinity College for the meagre few acres of stone and rushes and for the thatched damp cottage with flagstone floors in a central room and mud floors in a single bedroom. You were walking to Cavan, the journey of a full day, to pay rent in cash when you were a young girl and your father was ill and your mother unable to walk.

And what happened you between then and the time I met you I don't know. But life had not hardened you. That's the point, Alice.

Not even when you ended up in a damp abandoned cottage on the mountain with a thatched roof that fell in on one side, devastating the old kitchen, and leaving you with just a single room and a few sheets of tarpaulin to endure the winter.

That's when Eamonn heard of you and brought you to the parish house.

I've been through a few difficulties in the past year. I've had a few operations and I came here to the wild Atlantic coast to recuperate, and I have had that fog in the eye that closes you in, so I know a little about what I'm saying.

But I have never spent nights, never mind years, lying in a shed on straw, or lying under a fallen thatch, or sitting alone on a ditch with a cow. I've never known what it is to cling to a relationship with a cow as if she were mother and father, brother and sister.

I used to ask you about your brother and you'd just say, 'He's gone a long time,' with such sorrow that I couldn't bear to be further curious.

'And have you no one else?' I'd ask.

And you'd leave a silence. And then you'd whisper, 'No one.'

That could have left you bitter, or angry or coarse, or brutalised, or so I thought. But it didn't. Because I never met as gentle a woman, as soft and kind a hand on my head when you would reach out and caress it and then laugh, fingering my beard and muttering the words, 'Hairy Harding'.

So when Vincent arrived to the house in Leitrim with a copy of *The War on Dads and Children*, the book he had published and which *The Guardian* newspaper in Britain hailed as an important book about family law, my beloved phoned me and said there's someone here for you, and she put him on the phone and there I was all of a sudden talking again to Vincent. The same Vincent who was only about 12 years old when I was in Glangevlin, and must be in his sixties now, and I had not seen him since.

For a while I felt guilty. I'm only 20 minutes away from Glangevlin, and yet that drive up along the shores of the lake and through the village of Dowra always seemed too long. It was like driving into the past. Driving back decades to where I once was.

In the mid-'70s it was, in the hot summers that you loved because you could take off your winter coat and sit on the same ditch in a coloured cardigan that Eamonn gave you as a gift from his sister and because there were more people on the roads than in the bleak windy days of winter.

Tractors taking water up the hills to farmhouses in the

drought, and Joe McGovern fixing broken rakes and link boxes, and queues of young lads in wellingtons smoking cigarettes outside the garage, and me on the ditch with you, on my way home to the same august parish house we shared.

We talked about dancing and music and what tunes people played in the old days as you remembered them. Because back then we danced and sang and there was nothing else in our world. We didn't have instruments and we weren't among the important people of the world but we sang and we sang, without end. We danced half sets in the kitchens of the public houses and the mechanic's garage, and in Glangevlin Hall and in every pub from Blacklion to Dowra. We joked with guards on the way home when we saw their torches in the distance flagging us to slow down, with the shadow of soldiers in the ditches around them.

Just imagine! We were drunk, and smart-alecky with the police and yet they let us go. Back then drink didn't bother anyone as much. The police were looking for terrorists, for gunmen on the run. Although if we had known where they were hiding we would have said even less than nothing. Because the guards were not considered to be on our side. They were on the side of the state, the forces of law and order, and we inhabited a different space, where fun and love were the be-all and end-all of life.

Our world was a bubble of music that lasted till morning. It lasted until the fiddle player stopped. It lasted until we had gone through every Hank Williams record in the drawer to keep the kitchen dancing.

And I remember going back to the fiddle player's lovely house years later and finding that it was derelict, and so I went to his son's house but he too had died, and I asked a neighbour woman where his wife had gone, and she said that his wife too had gone to the grave.

In another house I saw a picture of the four of us – the son and his wife, me and Annie Joe – doing a half set, and you sitting on the wall with your stick and white hair, laughing at the laughter. The photograph was laminated and framed and hung so proudly on the wall. And even the man who took the photograph was in another graveyard somewhere else.

'The light of heaven to them all,' as you used to say.

And what is not in the photograph is the following day and the day after that. The endless days when I would meet you as I drove home from my teaching job in Loughan House and I'd get out of the car and sit on the ditch and smoke a cigarette as we conversed about the ancestry of humans, and the cures on the skin of animals, and the boys that used to throw water on the adults in the old sweathouses to cool them down.

I had nowhere to go, and I had all the time in the world, as they say, to idle the day.

'Well, master,' you would begin, just like Mickey Dominic, who always asked the same question at night in the pub to open up a conversation, 'what did you teach the young scholars today?'

You and Mickey Dominic came from the same cloth and time. When the poor went barefoot and envied the scholars and tried to gather a little learning on the ditches or at night in the rambling houses. Tried to gather a meaning for life from the scraps that fell from the mouths of the rich.

And that's where it always began with us. You would ask a question. You would set the agenda for our lovely conversation and we'd talk for an hour about dandelions, or ragwort or the power of healing in holy medals.

I felt we were like druids at the gates of the Christian monastery because it was usually just outside the priest's gates that we met, beside the pillar on the right-hand side.

I passed it recently and felt sad to see how it has deteriorated. I felt sad too to see that the fiddler's house is choked with ivy. And the schoolyard is empty and the roof fallen in and there are townlands you and me tried to figure out that are forgotten among the sitka forests. Townlands we chewed on, their names being embodied souls, their people being saints in a litany we recited. By naming things, we called them to mind. The forgotten townlands. The lost people. The abandoned cottages. The ones in England and America.

It was our ancient druidic ritual on the ditch, with my shining black and orange Ford Escort sitting idle at the turn.

But the thing is that when Vincent arrived on the bike from London he didn't know he was conjuring up again all your wonderful light. I wasn't even looking at him. He was just on the phone and he spoke fast and was hard to follow and the book, I said, the book, yes, I must read it. But when I put down the phone it was you that came to mind. Your angelic light brightening up the little house by the ocean. And when I opened the parcel that my beloved sent the following day, and saw the inscription on it, it was you clearly that had come into the house. 'To Hairy Harding', he wrote.

I belonged in those mountains. I belonged on that ditch. I belonged with you at my side and the dandelions growing wild around us. It wasn't just the nights of eternal joy that I found in the kitchens and pubs, and dancing half sets, but it was there with you, on the ditch, or on the sofa of the big kitchen, when you always asked me to tell you everything about last night's fun.

I think you relished the stories as if you had been there. I fancy they reminded you of some long-ago times when you were young and loved and full of fun. But if that's the case, you certainly kept it all to yourself.

You were a great woman for the long silence. You never spoke ill of anyone, but you could hold long silences that were devastating.

And when you didn't want to answer a question you were implacable. I would walk from one house to another on those evenings after parking my car at the priest's house. I would drop in to Phelim and watch the child on Kitty's knee; the child I spilled a cup of tea over when he was about three months old and caused such an almighty stir. Fortunately and thank God for me that the scalding tea left no scar, a fact the child assured me of when I met him in Drumshanbo 40 years later.

And then I'd pop into Lizzy James Hughie, from Armagh, who was married to Owenie and had a beautiful child at the kitchen table doing her homework. And finally on my route around the loop of Móinín Samhrain, the little bogs of the McGovern, I'd call in on Felix, a man who minded sheep on the mountains and read his way through philosophy books in winter, and I'd end up in a kitchen of a great musician who kept his ancestor's sword hanging on the wall. A weapon that belonged to a bishop who went over and back to Spain on trading ships in the eighteenth century studying theology, a time when a weapon was a necessary passport on the high seas. And those rambling afternoons full of music and history always ended in desire, when I was driving the young women to far-away dancehalls in Swanlinbar or Ballinamore or Drumshanbo.

The happiest years of your life, you would say to me. These are the happiest years of your life.

You were right. I would never have known the ordinariness of compassion or the casual ground of intimacy that is as natural to rural living as the soft rain and drizzle is to the hills above Blacklion. But it's your face, Alice, that remains. Your fogged eye and your clear blue and kindly eye. Your listening smile. Your soft wild white hair and the way you'd keep brushing it back from your face. Your sensual wide lips and the purple blotch just below your mouth. I remember it all.

As I remember the silence. As I remember lying awake sometimes pondering Eamonn's observation.

'She's an angel,' he would say.

And I know now that there are no accidents, Alice; not a leaf falls without it being willed by God.

He did everything he could to improve your conditions. He was blue in the face talking to people in the county council and the health board, to get you out of the shed with the cow. Eventually you agreed to a prefab and the council agreed to build it. You were slow to say yes, and difficult even when you had agreed to it.

'Where will I put Rabbit?' you wanted to know.

Eamonn said that Rabbit would still be in the shed and well fed and well sheltered and that the council could put the prefab up on the land just above the outhouses so that even if Rabbit did call for you in the night you would hear him.

It was the way we lived in those days. And so the prefab was erected and you were installed and the parish came to know it as Alice's prefab. It became a signpost on the road. If you were giving directions you might tell someone to turn left at Alice's prefab.

And you stood in the door, rotund, a blue cardigan draped on your stout shoulders, the stick in your hand, the white hair tidied up by a girl in Dowra who did all the women's hair; but you wouldn't let me in.

I could see from the door that the space within had been transformed into the chaos of the shed. The bed was hardly used. And the box stove was not lit. You were uneasy about lighting it.

'Me mother often said those things are not healthy,' you claimed.

I think about Glangevlin a lot and still marvel at the open-hearted way that people embraced me. But if there was a person then who remained in my memory as a single icon of that world it was you, because your life was the most rugged, and brutal, and impoverished. And yet your laughter was the most gentle. Your smile was the clearest and brightest. Your silence was the most inviting.

You went down to the pub for food very often and Mary or indeed anyone would gladly offer you a dinner. You belonged in the community and showed us a part of our invisible self.

How could that not be an accurate description of an angel?

I remember the day the prefab was dismantled. The council had it knocked, folded and up on the back of the lorry in less than an hour. All that remained was a cube of blackened earth within a patch of yellowed grass, and an empty gas cylinder. I stood on the black soil where no grass had grown and looked at the square of earth you had called home. There was something beautiful about the land all around, the rushes and the sally and ash trees, the roofs of the outhouses at the bottom of the hill, the crows that always congressed in the trees around that priest's house.

I remember it vividly as a sense of how little trace we leave on Earth. And while I remember that moment clearly, I have no recollection of your funeral or the passing of Rabbit the cow, who as far as I remember, from the folklore of the time, actually survived you and was cared for by the priest fondly until her time on Earth was over.

And I've said over and over again that the women in Glangevlin where a kind of collective mother to me. They minded me and taught me the importance of laughter, joy, intimacy and love.

But you were different. You were like the face of something deeply sacred. An enduring presence. A reassurance that, in someone who ought to have been brutalised by the hardships and injustices of life, you had retained a huge heart of kindness, gentleness and joy.

Words are beautiful and only true as far as they go; they only encompass the reality they name, so their effervescence and fragility is astonishing.

The poet's language flies like a bird, and the prose writer is surrounded by shot-down things that lie in sentences as flat as dead birds in a field.

And with the fragility of words, there is a way that grasping them chokes everything on the page.

Grasping a memory leads to acres of dead birds.

Enveloping the past in crimes that have wounded me, only hardens my heart to stone.

But Alice was like a word.

She was the embodiment of a sensibility that there was no name for. Her little stub nose and thick-set lips and foggy eye gave her the aspect of a buddha, and when she laughed her face broke open with joy. And when her hands moved from the stick, to the air, flapping like a bird as she described the colour of the night, it was like watching language take flesh. Each movement conveyed the steady immediacy of her presence. She was there with me then. And when I asked about Rabbit, the cow, she would bow her head as if like a clown she was mimicking sleep.

'Rabbit is sleeping,' I would conjecture.

And her head would nod. Rabbit was sleeping.

And even now when the stone comes into my mouth she takes it out, and when my tongue cannot form a word, I hear the silence speak.

FEBRUARY 2022

To an Old School Friend

Fuck it. What have I done? I feel I've wasted an entire year here at the ocean. Two months watching box sets, wearing pyjamas and listening to the wind howling.

Now it's February and my tooth almost fell out today. At least, an entire wall of it collapsed but the filling which was put in years ago remained intact.

I went to a dentist in Letterkenny who was kind enough to see me at short notice. She was a woman from eastern Europe and she said perhaps it would need to be taken out. Or at least the filling would come out and then she would have to do root canal work.

I just lay there on my back in her chair half terrified of the details and half happy that it was her because she seemed very competent and kind.

'So when do we begin?' I wondered, expecting that she'd have me back the following day.

'Maybe we will just wait and see what happens,' she said. 'There is a possibility that the filling will remain intact, and even though you lost some tooth, we might not need to do anything.'

Well, after showing me all the dangers first, I found this conclusion delightful. I walked out of the clinic as if I was walking on air.

'Just call if it gets worse or if you feel pain,' she said.

And here I am feeling no pain, feeling joyful, just because I didn't have to get my tooth out, just because I avoided root canal treatment for the moment. And I'm amazed at how simple life is.

No. How simple we are. How quickly we fall into heaven. How open we are to the prospect of angels, redemption, freedom, and second chances.

So that's when something washed away in me. Some sorrow that had clung to me all winter began to dissolve. It's as if I was waiting to be healed of stuff and yet I was nursing the wounds.

The operation last year has left me with an injured body. My bodily functions have been impaired. My retina has detached. And although fixed in January, the doctor says it will be another month before I recover sight in the left eye. It will require another procedure, he says, to sort out a cataract that has developed.

And I get weary thinking, wondering will it end. And then thinking that maybe it won't end; it will go on. If this doesn't get me, something else will, because I'm entering that time in life called old age.

'Don't let the old man in' is superbly true. But don't fool yourself either. He's out in the garden and someday he'll get you when you're not fucking looking.

But sure look, you have to remember, I did spend some time on the road as an actor. And you don't do that and survive unless you have a sense of humour. There's too much pain in the life of an actor, between the failed attempts to embody a narrative that gets rejected publicly over and over again. And if that is a bit like doing therapy in public, then there is also the vexed question of getting an audience.

'How many are in tonight?' every actor wants to know in the waiting moments that she or he spends in the green room before the lights go up.

I remember one of the most painful moments happened me in Kilmallock.

I arrived on a wet Saturday afternoon and presented myself to a member of the amateur drama company who was clearing away the flats from the previous night's production of a play by John B. Keane.

'It went fantastically well,' he said. 'They were hanging from the rafters, and they nearly broke themselves with laughter. We'll have to bring it back again in a week or two.'

I was carrying my bench, the one I used in that production of *Swallow*. I carried it like the lid of a coffin and asked him if he or someone else was doing the lights for the show later that evening.

'I didn't know there was anything on tonight,' he said, a bit confused, 'but I'll ring the director and she can sort you out.'

So he phoned the woman who ran the theatre and I sat in the back row of the hall waiting for her to ring me. Maybe they forgot I was coming. Or maybe a brief 25-minute show, involving a man standing on a bench with a sad little poster proclaiming the show to have been a hit at the Dublin Fringe Festival, wasn't a great enticement to the people of Kilmallock. Perhaps having seen a lively Keane play on the Friday night they weren't going to be enticed back again on a wet Saturday in November.

One way or another, it became clear when the lady who ran the theatre arrived that something was wrong. The chairman of her committee was with her, and she confessed after a lot of whispering with him in her office that in fact they had no bookings.

No bookings. Like – no bookings at all.

'We'd be better to shift the performance to the rehearsal room upstairs,' she said.

And I wondered like, why? If there's no bookings. That's the bit I could never understand. I wanted to say it might be better not to put it on if there was no audience, but I was innocent and had no manager and feared my fee might dissolve into the same place the audience were hanging out.

Nowhere.

So I agreed to put the show on at the appointed hour in the rehearsal room upstairs. And I know I should have discussed the money. I should have known that I could have called on a guarantee. But back then it wasn't like that. I was innocent, and so were they. We were all amateurs, to an extent. And like the naive presumption that there is a God, we both presumed that since I was there, the show must go on. The only problem was how to create an audience.

The chairman of the committee mustered ten chairs, and five of them were taken as the play began. One of them was the lighting man from the amateur drama society whom I had met earlier, one was the woman who ran the venue, and one was the chairman, who fell asleep even in the brief time that I was on the bench, confessing the private grief of a Monaghan farmer as if it were my own. And even the script didn't shelter me from the shame and the humiliation I was feeling as I stood on the bench, playing my part; I was like a child in a classroom being tortured by the world.

Maybe it wasn't even the drama on stage that I relished when I was touring. Maybe it was the other dramas – the ones off stage – that I loved. My grandfather was a pig dealer. He walked the streets of every Ulster town from Cavan to Belfast and visited every fair from Coleraine to Armagh, in search of animals he would purchase and put on trains to Cavan. And he would come home triumphant on the last train after weeks on the road with the money in his boot.

I felt him sitting in the back seat of the car when I was on the road because I too loved the road: the flavours of different towns, the ease of always being a stranger just arrived.

I remember once on the street in Tralee looking into a shop window full of Hallowe'en ghouls in black and orange when a man stood behind me and commented on the play I had performed the night before in Siamsa Tíre.

'It was a great performance last night,' the man said, 'and I enjoyed it.'

I said, 'Thank you. What's your name?'

'Sullivan,' he said. Sullivan from Tiranee.

He gave no Christian name. Just his family handle, and the place that he came from. I hadn't a clue where Tiranee was, but I understood the connection between identity and location in rural Ireland.

And what about the time I was in the bath in the Clarion Hotel in Limerick, just hours before the opening, playing with bath gels and sachets of expensive shampoo, when the phone rang.

It was a teacher at the prison, with a request. Would I meet the prisoners? I agreed to go to the prison because that was the best thing about being on the road as an actor.

It wasn't the acting or the play or the performance that excited me. It was simply being on the road and hearing more stories.

So I said yes to the prison. Perhaps because I was in good mood, on the first day of the tour, and the hotel to me, a struggling actor, appeared luxurious and I wasn't thinking of the reality that I myself would be paying for it, and perhaps too because the teacher on the phone from the prison was so complimentary about my acting, and said she often saw me in plays in Dublin, and would it be awful for her to ask me to come and talk to the prisoners. Not at all, I declared majestically, from my little world of bubbles. Glad to oblige.

I was expansive and exuberant and naked, and for some reason felt like James Bond, or Pierce Brosnan, or both, and perhaps she will bring other teachers and prison staff to the play, I thought, if I visit the prison.

'You're someone different,' she said. 'It's important for them sometimes to meet someone different. To be able to talk to someone different.'

'We can pay you,' she said.

'How much?'

'Two hundred euro.'

I almost dropped my mobile into the ocean of bubble bath. But the deal was done.

The following morning I was at the prison gates at nine o'clock, standing in the rain, waiting for her to arrive and lead me through the various doors and security checks.

By ten o'clock I'm inside, listening to prisoners and hoping to find a connection between their stories, and whatever it is I do every night on the stages of the nation.

I was staring at this woman who reminded me of a nun, in her grey cardigan and her eyes like pinpoints behind steel-rimmed glasses. We were in the small, fully fitted kitchen of the women's unit of the prison. It could have been her home were it not for the double-plated glass wall through which I could see other women playing pool and a fat prison officer with a beer belly and his cap pushed back on his head sitting in the corner reading yesterday's *Evening Herald*.

For years, before she was convicted of dealing in serious drugs, this woman kept hens and guinea pigs and rabbits in her back garden, in the working-class estate where she lived, so that the children of the street could come and enjoy them, like rich children did when they went to the zoo in Dublin.

She told me about all the pets she ever had. And how she loved them. And how the house would be full of children, always coming to see her crazy zoo. She had an owl that ate live mice. And a jackdaw that went to school with her daughter.

She told me that she loved animals as a child, and that she could remember the day her father abandoned her. He left from the station. She went with him hand in hand, and he lifted her up in the sky, and his arms were big like lumps of trees, and the plume of white steam from the train enveloped them on the platform so she thought she was in clouds going to heaven.

But only her father went, and, she suspected, not to heaven. After some years his place was taken by her mother's new lover, whom she never liked. So she spent her youth in the fields, talking to the donkey. Until one day she went out and the donkey was dead. Its throat had been cut in the night.

She looked out at me from behind the glasses, as if she were a mouse looking out from the safety of a dark cavern. She wore her story like a shell. She was safe so long as she stayed inside it. Her bony face never flinched. Her fist was always clenched on the table. She had no intention of telling me how she felt inside.

The teacher and I then walked across the yard, beneath a huge 20-foot stone wall, to the next building. The male prison.

Inside we met a good-looking man of about 45 years, in the pool room, who was stressed and edgy. Once again, the teacher introduced me as an actor and a friend, and we stopped for a few moments to chat, and once again he grasped the moment with all his might.

Just a kind of grey lightness in the air, and the smell of stale cigarettes, and the game of pool, for a moment frozen in time, as the other players waited and witnessed, and he spoke his story with his hands still, his head bowed, his voice clear.

Over the pool table, he talked about long-ago times in the country, when a wet day was known as haircut day. Because there was nothing to do, everybody would congregate in his father's house, and his father would cut everybody's hair.

One day he was idling in the kitchen and all the men's hair had been cut, and there was still more rain lashing down outside and his father looked at him and pointed the scissors at the kitchen chair.

'Might as well do you too,' he said to the boy. But the boy would have none of it, for he loved his long curls, and he ran out the door, his father on his heels, cursing and roaring in rage at the child's disobedience.

Two hours later his father fell dead as he pumped the wheel of the bike in the shed. A massive heart attack, the men of the haircuts declared to the boy, as they carried the corpse on the back of a door out the laneway to the waiting ambulance.

For some reason I felt like breaking the snooker cue in two across his head. 'There's no connection,' I said. 'You did not cause your father's death.'

'I know,' he said, 'I know. But sure, that's my story. And I'll have to live with it.'

He was neither lying nor acting. This is who I am, he was telling me, in this myth, in this pool game. This is me. This is my mask.

I was dazed as I left the prison in the early afternoon and crossed the wet and windy streets of the city towards my hotel. To be able to step out on the street was a sweet sensation after speaking with people who cannot step into a toilet in the next ten years without permission. But to walk out onto the stage in the Belltable that night, after witnessing their wounded lives embodied in the simplicity of their own stories, was an act that seemed beyond all rational explanation. Either it was an act of shameful self-promotion, or it was a miracle.

Despite all my failures on the stage and in life, I still opted to hope it was the latter. I believe in miracles. We all do. We who go again into the same space, in the hope of the same outcome that we never quite achieve.

Once more, as we say, jokingly, unto the breach.

So here's what I've learned. That every time I think I have shaped the narrative of meaning, it blows up in my face. Every time I tunnel into my little world of icons and gods and prayers, it dissolves in my hands. Every time I think I know the past and feel remorse for all the things I did badly, there is some angel comes and says stop making a fuss of yourself.

I'll put it in terms that Rumi might use. When I walk towards God, God runs towards me. The veil of the world distances me from God, but it doesn't distance God from me. God is closer to me than I am to myself, and that's why all my sense of identity, narrative, of being me, cracks and crumbles under the pressure of something so close to me that I can't name it.

If I said it was God, then I would have to say that's the wrong answer. And my conclusion is that there is no conclusion. And then I ask myself why was I here for an entire year, like a monk with candles and icons and looking out the window at the sea and talking to people who are long dead.

And the answer is that I don't know. And when I get to that discombobulation, and when the house of meaning falls down around me, I am left naked, with a sore tooth, with a pain in the arse, and an overwhelming desire to walk on the beach. Why? Because there is no reason to walk on the beach. And I'm still alive and lucky enough to be here living the life that has no meaning.

So the broken tooth nearly finished me.

Like, think about it again: I've had colitis, a mental breakdown, an operation on the prostate, a heart attack, a detached retina and two spinal operations to correct an AE fistula.

And then what happens? My fucking tooth breaks. Well, my gosh, there's the tragedy. I could live with the rest but don't take my tooth out.

So when the dentist said let's leave it and see what happens it was like she was giving me the gift of life.

It was difficult to contain the joy.

What am I saying? I'm saying the winter is washing off me. I am still here at the ocean. I can walk and talk and see and hear. I am alive in this moment and it's so fucking beautiful I can't think what veil could possibly exist now between heaven and me.

Is that just the days getting longer?

Probably.

Soon I will phone you. Soon I will invite you to come up for a few days. Soon the beloved lady wife will come too and we will all walk on the beach together. Wouldn't that be a great idea for the spring days ahead?

APRIL 2022

To a Lover

One night we slept together in sleeping bags and snuggled up like one thing on the floor.

I thought our sleep would mingle like the smoke of single candles and waft into an ecstasy of silence and abandonment.

I thought that if we floated down below the line of consciousness, then the corals of the ocean's floor would be mysteries that we could share forever.

I watched you with your eyelids locked, drifting in and out of nothing; and totally yourself. And I saw you smiling inwardly at prizes even then I didn't share.

You shivered once and suddenly were upright and unzipped. Setting out for water in the kitchen.

That was around 3 a.m. I saw the time in digits on the clock and I saw your brittle breaking loose from sleep like a forceful defiance, like a duck clattering to be up above the waves, and your powerful determination made me hope I had another chance.

But afterwards you pulled the bag across your shoulders and went off again, with the rim of it tucked under your chin like the walls of Troy.

I had failed before we even began. But I know now you are not a bird, a fish or even Helen, as you eased away mysteriously from everyone.

In sleep you abandon the world. A letting go of all your loves, to find a deeper one. And sleep inhabits you and steers you out to hiding places in the ocean I can never know.

I watch abandoned at the harbour, as your breathing rises, to an even swell, and I cling to the harbour wall like a barge, on the stillness of the night.

Who I write to is not a rational choice. And who surfaces in my memory is not rational either. I'm aware of that every time my mother returns to haunt me.

But there are other ghosts. Like the 12 men that sit on stools around the walls of the kitchen. They walked out of my beloved's dream and entered the house, and now they sit silent all the time like a chorus.

And there are ghosts of the future that I consider angels; they reach back into time, to recast me in their image so that I can become as beautiful as them.

They are angels that raise me to the condition of icon, and I sing with them in the morning: 'Holy, holy, holy art thou, O blessed and beloved one.'

And as spring turns to summer again, I find myself satisfied corresponding with the dead. With people who have passed away and are wrapped in memories and float up in the dark before me as I make my confession and ask their forgiveness. And now all that is for me to do is gather up those letters, like prayers, and light a fire on the beach and shred each one so that the smoke rises into the wind like an offering, a puja, a song of love and regret.

I found you, like someone come to save me.

I found you like a deep sanctuary lamp at the corner of a cloister, in the distance, like some safe zone I could travel to. I found you like a peaceful field, inside my heart.

We climbed into bed together and lay motionless, staring at the ceiling and sometimes at each other.

If we had touched or made love I might not have remembered so intensely. But the consequences of abstaining on that precipice of desire, when we were both young and no one was watching, have been enormous.

Only the moonlight in the room, that white ghostly glow

that was strong enough to throw shadows on the floor, only that light made me feel like someone was watching.

But the other guests were gone to bed. The other artists. The other residents. The other travellers. All were sleeping, and you and I were keeping watch in the night; watching each other and wondering what comes next.

Well, let me tell you I'm grateful for every step that followed.

I suppose at the time I didn't know how significant that transgression would be for the rest of my life. But now I must tell you. The enormity of that encounter, and the transformative consequences for our friendship.

It's almost like lovemaking destroys friendship in the forge and creates a new thing called love. To do it idly is to blaspheme. To do it casually or often is to diminish the power of language and the power of embodiment. Until in the end the human who has so used their language of love ends up dismembered, disembodied, like a ghost talking by rote, and finding that more and more repetitions offer only less and less.

Lovemaking can only work if it is the sacrament. The ultimate sacrament.

So at the time I longed for completion beneath your blankets but I was filled with fantasies. I thought sex would offer me a sense of triumph and conquest. I may have even held back because you held back. I may have been a coward. You may have been too beautiful with your curling black hair. You may have frightened me.

We were so close, and yet you held back.

So I held back.

Or maybe you held back because I held back. Who knows?

Maybe there was a barrier of inhibition and repression and fear between us. Or some force field of opposites in the universe, made manifest in our bodies, that held us apart. Something that created a film of separation, because something most certainly held us apart, yet close together. A kind of link possessed us. And made one of us, in our immobility.

I didn't choose to go to bed with you that night. I certainly didn't choose to lie all night at such a distance from you.

But there was a lightness when we woke in the morning and rushed for our clothes like Adam and Eve to eat breakfast in quiet modesty with the kitchen table between us.

I went on the back road behind the sand dunes of Machaire Uí Rabhartaigh beach, because it was so windy that I thought my hat wouldn't stay on if I walked by the shore.

And after an hour walking I climbed one of the sand dunes at the very end of the beach. This is the place from where I can look out to Toraigh Island and remember that Colmcille walked along this same beach and wrote poetry about the beaches of Donegal. And out there on the island is the Tau, the last letter of the Aramaic alphabet, as like the omega in Greek, the final completion of the universe that comes in Christ, or so Colmcille believed.

I knew instantly that I was destined to be a solitary pilgrim, no matter what path I chose in life, and yet the future was bright. The day was luminous. The kitchen window was enormous, and the sunlight fell on your curling hair and silenced me like a flickering candle can silence a monk in his cell for years.

We even laughed. Maybe to hide our failures. Our lack of sophistication. To protect our dignity and mask whatever disfunction had been exposed.

Was it damage in you that I woke? Or would you presume it was damage in me that made us lie perversely chaste, resisting sex in the world where young people had so much permission to be young and be in bed. We slept so long that night, and yet stayed awake forever, both truly desiring the other and tasting the desire in each other for so long that it felt like an eternity.

And when the moon went down the sun came up.

What held us back?

Even at breakfast the following morning I had begun to mythologise it. Could it be that your loneliness cried out so much to mine that you feared that a new life would change you too much? Could it be that my loneliness cried out so strong that I too feared a new life would destroy me? Destroy the old me. Because that is what happens in love. It destroys who you thought you were. It destroys who you really were. It remakes you as a package with the other. As a player of love songs on a stage where the other is a constant absence that fills you entirely. And so it is here on this beach, on this sand dune, looking out at the islands of Bó Finne and Toraigh. Here in this place your absence matters and the place matters.

But theology doesn't matter. The intellectual constraints that bound Colmcille in his soul and for his entire life to the rocks of Donegal don't matter.

It is the fact that he lived here and walked here that counts; and practised in the same tradition as any meditator whether they be Christian, Buddhist,

Islamic, Sufi, Kaballistic or aficionados of modern mindfulness. They're all the same.

He practised love, as a kind of knowing, and from this fountain flowed such energy that a thousand monasteries and a thousand beautiful embroidered books of love were created.

Who am I to walk on the beach and not remember him? What diminishment to humans would that be, if I forgot Jerusalem as it was built out there on Toraigh Island.

Toraigh and Bó Finne. The Tau as the eschatological masculine and Bó Finne as the cosmic mother.

We knew each other's brokenness before we began. And by the time the night had ended we had seen each other's wounds. And in the wound some enormous light was coming through and neither of us wanted it.

Not this intensity, we seemed to whisper. This will be too much. It will destroy who we are, and ruin our friendship and we will have to remake the world again, with each other, and that could take years.

Who wants that?

Let me just be me and fuck you, and leave it at that.

I am sure now, after all these years, that you were sent to me. That the moment of intimacy in your bed that night did in fact last a lifetime. All the lovemaking that followed could not be put in seven volumes. But what remains exquisite is the memory of that first single moment. When we were both on the threshold. And we both said no, not now, it's too much. And then, and then … we said yes.

And when we parted the following day, after breakfast, on the platform of the train station, I told you myself that I had met an angel.

I held your body close to mine, inhaled your perfume, the self-folds of your mohair jumper in rainbow colours, and the fragrance from the back of your neck where my cheek rested as we hugged; we kissed on the cheek as the train pulled in, four times, and at last, just once our lips came close, imbued with all the possibilities anyone could dream up. The train stopped. I got on and looked out the window and waved. It was a perfect railway station farewell.

No one must ever know of your love. That felt like the condition on which it would begin. I went off on the train and you went back to your room and we had time to say farewell to the old lives, before our next meeting. Before we stepped into Paradise together.

And sometimes here in Donegal I walk to the headland alone and watch the foam ripping away from the great waves as the wind comes from the south, and I watch the white breakers on the rocks, and see the light in mighty shafts breaking the clouds and making the far horizon of the ocean glitter with silver, and I see you again. I see you here, in the depth of it all. And I can tell you and show you now this day that I am here.

I am present.

When I was young we called it love. And I said I love the blackbird. I said I love the begonia. I love the rose and I love the trees. I could sit for hours under the oak or beech. I could sit there and feel loved. More closely and more spontaneously than a mother's love.

But the ocean is different. It's frightening. Its presence is not like an oak tree. When you meet the sea, you have met everyone. And your knots are loosened. What frightens me is that there's nothing human about it at all, unless by human you understand it as the embodiment of the invisible, the icon of the angelic realm that is all about us, singing in the wind and in the cawing of gulls and the little squeaks of the wren in the furze.

The letters had been remembrance, but the journey of life is a kind of forgetting.

There was no naming my condition. Call it joy. Call it heaven, if you like. It was like experiencing a magnificent full moon or hearing a bird sing or noticing the complexity on the wings of a moth.

The entire year had been a ritual of remembrance. A recitation of love and regret. The previous days had been hot and dry. Now it was soft and misty. I sat in a blustery heaven and wondered, suddenly, where and why and to whom do I say the word Beloved.

EPILOGUE

To an Old School Friend

I said I would phone you and so I will; we will meet again, in the summer, you and me and the beloved. We will walk along the beach.

In the meantime you are wondering why I wrote to you. We are not close. We cling to memories and record the deaths of old classmates as we might mark milestones on a journey, but we don't have any other connection.

And the thing about the dead is that no one remembers them for long. Life goes forward. The living stand supreme because every new morning they get another chance to love.

I could have chosen others to write to. It's part of growing old that you begin to know more and more dead people. I could have picked others who are just as important to me. I could have picked people to whom I owe apologies for wrongs I committed. Others from whom I might have begged forgiveness. People to whom I am grateful for guiding me. And those so beautiful and bright that my heart was made glad by just thinking about them.

They are all gone and their eyes will never open again and they will never read what I write, or never speak what they feel. They are gone.

But you hear me. You read me. You feel what you feel because you are alive.

Dermot Healy opened my heart to poetry. Pat O'Brien drew me into the ways of philosophy. Tom Hickey inspired me to work in theatre. Bernard Loughlin encouraged me to trust my artistic gift.

And Mary McPartlan was like a sister, so intimately engaged with life that I fell into good humour every time I saw her smiling face.

And at our marriage, Bernard was first in the door of the church, though his faith was not conventional, Tom was best man, Mary was best woman, and Pat conducted the religious ceremony. And all are gone now, three taken in almost the space of a year.

But they were not alone. Almost everyone I met has been a helper. Every new person marks a turning point. So then what are we supposed to do when the ones we love suddenly slip into the shadows to join the vague amorphous company of the ancestors?

I'm nearly 70 years old. And I'm writing to you because I

begin to feel good about this sublime transience. Knowing how ordinary we are, and how short life is, brings a kind of peace and an overwhelming sense of gratitude.

It's an insight that allows me to pray with the ancestors, as well as write letters to them. It allows me to feel that all those loved ones beyond my fingertips still endure in an altered form; I sense they are absorbed into the ineffable mystery of being.

My faith or my imagination, or both, allow me to say I will meet Tom again. And Mary. And Bernard. And Pat. And the child with the blue shoe will look me in the eye. And Alice will see me again with her heart.

There is no getting away from our responsibilities. Our lives are a series of actions, and every action has its consequences.

And it's funny how we never expect people to die. We certainly don't expect that we might have to face the same darkness.

Let me tell you how unexpected it was with Dermot. We were in the Model Arts and Niland Gallery in Sligo a few years ago, at a charity event that Dermot had helped organise.

The final act was a local jazz band and they were playing the last set when Dermot, being full of exuberance, left his seat and began an impromptu dance at the foot of the stage. I was in the front row. And when the music stopped he went to go, and I called his name and he turned and said, 'I'll talk to you later.'

Then he vanished into the dark abyss on stage right, and as it happened, I never saw him again.

But I hear him yet, when the geese in autumn travel across Arigna on their way to Wexford.

And on the lush pathways around Glenveagh National Park I meet Bernard Loughlin and hear him in the shadows muttering admiration for the splendour of delphiniums.

There are certain love songs I cannot hear without imagining Mary McPartlan's voice phrasing every word, somewhere out there in the dark, on her way home.

Pat O'Brien I often meet at the entrance to various churches, graveyards and holy wells. He's always lingering just outside the door, or the gate, smoking a cigarette and leaning on a wall, and calling my attention to the fact that God is everywhere.

And as for Alice, well, it's funny that I should write to her, since she couldn't read nor see, but I might read it to her aloud sometime to make her smile when we are both on the ditches of heaven's idle meadows. And certainly I can never pass through Glangevlin without expecting to see her wave from the side of the road.

As Mickey Dominic used to say to me about the ancestors that went before him – they are all in heaven now.

And I believe it is not just because faith in God is the foundation of poetry, but also because as we age, the sense of something beneath the transient tide of life awakens in us, the sense that there is some depth of meaning in all this chaos cries out to us. It breaks us away from the living and aligns us not with the dead but in a new realm of love.

Although for the moment, you and I are here. And as long as we live, almost everything is still possible. So don't grieve. As Rumi says, anything you lose comes back in another form.

And may you live forever.

And expect a phone call.

Soon.

Acknowledgements

I am indebted to my agent, Marianne Gunn O Connor, for making this book possible. And to my editor, Ciara Doorley, for guiding me and inspiring me in the shaping of it.

My thanks as ever to Cathy, without whose encouragement, love and support this work would not be possible.

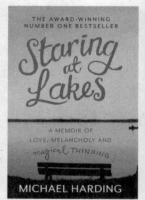

THE AWARD-WINNING
NUMBER ONE BESTSELLER

Staring
at
Lakes

A MEMOIR OF
LOVE, MELANCHOLY, AND
magical THINKING

MICHAEL HARDING

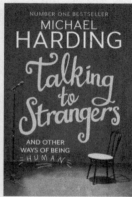

NUMBER ONE BESTSELLER

MICHAEL
HARDING

Talking
to
Strangers

AND OTHER
WAYS OF BEING
HUMAN

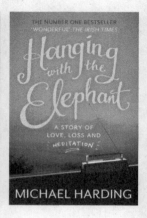

THE NUMBER ONE BESTSELLER
'WONDERFUL' THE IRISH TIMES

Hanging
with the
Elephant

A STORY OF
LOVE, LOSS AND
MEDITATION

MICHAEL HARDING

THE NUMBER ONE BESTSELLING AUTHOR

MICHAEL
HARDING

What is
Beautiful
in the Sky

A MEMOIR ABOUT ENDINGS
AND BEGINNINGS

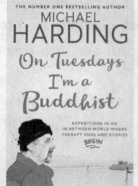

THE NUMBER ONE BESTSELLING AUTHOR

MICHAEL
HARDING

On Tuesdays
I'm a
Buddhist

EXPEDITIONS IN AN
IN-BETWEEN WORLD WHERE
THERAPY ENDS AND STORIES
BEGIN

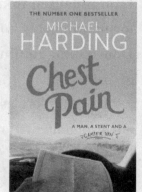

THE NUMBER ONE BESTSELLER

MICHAEL
HARDING

Chest
Pain

A MAN, A STENT AND A
CAMPER VAN

In this stunning collaboration, bestselling writer Michael Harding's most memorable musings on the human condition are brought to life by illustrator Jacob Stack.

In these pages, the reader is held in moments of belonging, solitude, love and healing as we witness the beauty of falling snow, the pain and love of goodbyes, and the shared lives and deaths of neighbours amid the sweeping landscape of Ireland.

A Cloud Where the Birds Rise is a beautifully illustrated collection of observations and stories from one of Ireland's best-loved writers – a celebration of finding beauty and hope in the ordinary.